Growing in CHRIST®

Upper Elementary Teacher Guide

CONCORDIA PUBLISHING HOUSE · SAINT LOUIS

God Creates a World and a People

OLD TESTAMENT 1

Copyright © 2006, 2007, 2016 Concordia Publishing House
3558 S. Jefferson Avenue, St. Louis, MO 63118-3968
1-800-325-3040 • www.cph.org

All rights reserved. Unless specifically noted, no part of this publication may be reproduced, stored in a retrieval system, or transmitted, in any form or by any means, electronic, mechanical, photocopying, recording, or otherwise, without the prior written permission of Concordia Publishing House.

The purchaser of this publication is allowed to reproduce the marked portions contained herein for use with this curriculum. These resources may not be transferred or copied to another user.

Written by Cynthia Schilf, Julie Stiegemeyer, and Deborah Henry

Edited by Deborah Henry, Thomas A. Nummela, and Lisa M. Clark

Unless otherwise indicated, all Scripture quotations are from the ESV® Bible (The Holy Bible, English Standard Version®), copyright © 2001 by Crossway, a publishing ministry of Good News Publishers. Used by permission. All rights reserved.

Catechism quotations are from *Luther's Small Catechism with Explanation*, copyright © 1986, 1991 Concordia Publishing House.

The quotations from Luther's Works in this publication are from the American Edition: vol. 4 © 1964 Concordia Publishing House; vol. 5 © 1968 by Concordia Publishing House. All rights reserved.

Manufactured in the United States of America

Growing in Christ® is published quarterly by Concordia Publishing House. Your comments and suggestions concerning this material are appreciated. Email us at sundayschool@cph.org.

Contents

Lesson	Title	Page	Date of Use
	Introduction	5	
1	God Creates the World	7	_____
2	God Creates Adam and Eve	15	_____
3	Sin Enters the World	23	_____
4	Cain and Abel	29	_____
5	Noah and the Flood	37	_____
6	God's Covenant with Abram	45	_____
7	Abraham's Visitors from Heaven	53	_____
8	Abraham and Isaac	61	_____
9	Isaac and Rebekah	69	_____
10	Jacob and Esau	77	_____
11	Jacob's Dream	83	_____
12	Jacob's Family	91	_____
13	Esau Forgives Jacob	99	_____
	Resource Pages	109	

Introduction

The Upper Elementary level of the **Growing in Christ** curriculum is generally intended for use with students who are in third through fifth grades. Depending on the maturity of your students, it can also be used with younger or older students. The materials for this level include a Teacher Guide, a set of Teacher Tools, and a Student Pack. The materials for this level have been designed for easy preparation and instruction. Check out these resources.

Features of the Teacher Guide

The thirteen lessons in this guide are organized into four steps.

- **Opening**—including worship and routine Sunday School housekeeping
- **God Speaks**—the Bible study
- **We Live**—in-depth application of God's Word and the Lutheran doctrines for the students' lives
- **Closing**—review and closing devotions

Every lesson has an initial page offering "Preparing the Lesson" commentary about the scriptural text and a reproducible page to be used at some point in the lesson. The additional resource pages at the end of the guide provide portions of the Small Catechism, a glossary listing the Faith Words to be taught, and directions for all games used in the quarter. All reproducible pages are found in PDF files on the Teacher CD. The perforated pages of the guide make it adaptable for other teaching scenarios, such as team teaching or substituting.

Teacher Tools

This packet contains essential tools for teaching a full lesson. Each quarter includes these items.

- **Faith Word Cards**—Interwoven in the lessons are four lesson-specific faith vocabulary words. Use these cards in a variety of ways to help instill the language of the faith.
- **Bible Review Cards**—These cards contain questions, numbered according to their level of difficulty, relating to the Bible account. The set contains eight cards per lesson (104 total). Use these cards for review during the quarter or with the review games described in the Teacher Guide. Save the cards from each quarter to continue the review process and to play review games during the entire year.
- **Growing in Christ Puzzle Book**—These puzzles are designed to assist the students in learning a key Bible verse or essential concepts from the lesson.
- **Timeline Poster**—This poster details the period of biblical history from which the quarter's lessons are drawn and points out significant events in world history.
- **Other Posters**—Additional posters explore various aspects of Lutheran doctrine.
- **CD**—This contains audio recordings of hymns, several of the weekly Bible Words, several portions of Luther's Small Catechism set to music, melody-line scores for all the music in PDF files, lyrics for the hymns and songs in RTF format, and PDF files of the reproducible pages from the Teacher Guide. The Bible Words and catechism recordings are tools designed to help your students learn these important texts. You have permission to copy the reproducible pages, scores, and lyrics to use in class. **Recorded music is not reproducible.** If you wish to copy it, contact CPH copyrights office by emailing copyrights@cph.org or by calling 1-800-325-0191.

Student Pack

Each quarter, this packet of materials contains two items.

- **Lesson Leaflets**—Nested in a self-cover (designed for students to take home and use as a poster) are thirteen four-page leaflets, one for each week of the quarter.
- **Bible Discovery Guide**—This combined atlas, dictionary, and encyclopedia of biblical information is compiled specifically for the lessons in this quarter. Almost every week, the students will reference the wide variety of information provided in illustrations and text to learn more about the Bible account. Students will want to keep this book as a future reference, but it should be stored at church so the students have them each week. Later, send it home for future reference.

Additional Materials

Classrooms should have some basic teaching equipment and materials available each week: Bibles, catechisms, hymnals, songbooks, CD player, pencils or pens, paper, index cards, crayons or markers, tape, scissors, glue, and a chalkboard, whiteboard, or newsprint pad with chalk or markers.

You may wish to order the following helps from Concordia Publishing House (browse cph.org, or call 1-800-325-3040 for subscription information and to order):

- *My Devotions*—Daily devotions for families with children eight to thirteen years old
- *Bible Story Posters*—Set of thirteen biblical art posters for the lessons in this quarter
- *Church Year Connections*—Tips and resources for teaching your students about the Church Year and connecting to the three-year lectionary
- **Arch Books**—CPH has these books that relate to Bible accounts this quarter; use them for Bible story presentation or review, or have them available before class.

Lesson 1	*Where Did the World Come From?*	59-2239
Lesson 2	*The Story of Creation*	59-1560
Lesson 3	*Falling into Sin*	59-2287
	From Adam to Easter	59-2265
Lesson 4	*Cain and Abel*	59-2283
Lesson 5	*Noah's 2-by-2 Adventure*	59-1511
	A Man Named Noah	59-2206
Lesson 6	*Abraham, Sarah & Isaac*	59-2244
Lesson 7	*Abraham, Sarah & Isaac*	59-2244
Lesson 8	*Abraham's Big Test*	59-1502
Lesson 11	*Jacob's Dream*	59-1538

Teaching Helps

You can find many teaching helps, including updates, training helps, and links to podcasts and other resources for your weekly preparation and teaching, at our Sunday School website, cph.org/sundayschool.

UPPER ELEMENTARY

Preparing the Lesson

God Creates the World

Genesis 1:1–2:3

Lesson 1

Date of Use

Key Point

God made the world in six days by the power of His Word. All creation is God's blessing to us.

Law/**Gospel**

God requires that I believe that He is the only true God, the Creator and Sustainer of the world. **God gives me faith to believe that He created the earth and heavens, and He continues to provide me with all that I need to sustain this body and life, including forgiveness for my sins, through His Son, Jesus Christ.**

Context

Genesis is a family history about Abraham, Isaac, and Jacob (called Israel), chosen by God. The creation account and other material in Genesis 1–11 serves as foundation for the family history that follows in Genesis 12–50.

Moses is the authority behind the first five books of the Bible, called the Torah (Law). Some material was revealed directly to Moses; other material was known to generations before Moses and, under the guidance of the Holy Spirit, was set down by him or immediate successors.

The Genesis accounts of creation, the preflood world, the flood, and the immediate resettlement after the flood have parallels in ancient writings that predate Moses, particularly in Mesopotamia.

Commentary

The Spirit of God hovering over the waters of the formless void shows that the Spirit brings order out of chaos. This image recurs in the Baptism of Christ (Mark 1:10), where it reminds us that in Christ we are a new creation (2 Corinthians 5:17), with the Spirit bringing order out of our chaos. The Hebrew word translated "Spirit" in Genesis 1:2 also means "wind" or "breath."

Words are formed from breath. As God proceeds to speak creation into being, the Genesis account establishes a unity between God the speaker, the Word by which He created the world, and the Spirit. This Word became flesh in Christ Jesus, as proclaimed in John 1:1–14. The words of Psalm 104:30 also portray the Spirit as an agent of creation. God's Word does what it says ("Let there be . . . and there was"). What God declares is true; God's Word is truth (John 17:17).

God begins His creation by creating light on the first day. God is the real source of light. Each day, God adds dramatically to the world that He calls "good"—heaven; earth and seas; plants; sun, moon, and stars; creatures that swim and fly; creatures that walk and crawl on the ground; and finally, man, both male and female. Some mistakenly worship the sun or other elements of creation that merely do what God assigns to them. However, they were not made to be worshiped but to be used.

The creation of people on the sixth day serves as the climax of creation. God creates both male and female in His image. Our image is not physical likeness but spiritual likeness, or righteousness. Note that man's rule over all other creatures and marriage/procreation are part of the sinless creation, which God declares "very good." God gives plants as food; death for humans and animals is not part of this perfect creation. Everything is intended to work for good.

Because God rested on the seventh day (our Saturday), the Sabbath ("rest") day was set apart ("made holy"). The ceremonial laws regarding the Sabbath have their fulfillment in Christ, who, having finished His work on Good Friday (John 19:30), rested in the tomb on the Sabbath. Christians from the earliest times met on Sundays to celebrate His resurrection. The commandment concerning the Sabbath no longer pertains to a particular day of the week but rather to setting aside time so that God might re-create us through His Word. Creation's patterns give us a sense of how things "ought to be."

To hear an in-depth discussion of this Bible account, visit cph.org/podcast and listen to our Seeds of Faith podcast each week.

Lesson 1

God Creates the World

Genesis 1:1–2:3

Connections

Bible Words
By [Christ] all things were created, in heaven and on earth, visible and invisible. Colossians 1:16

Faith Words
create, triune, Bible, testament

Hymn
Thy Strong Word (*LSB* 578; CD 7)

Catechism
Apostles' Creed: First Article (CD 16–20)

Liturgy
The Invocation

Teacher Tip
Establish classroom rules as you begin the year, and repeat them frequently. Keep them simple; limit the number of rules to about five.

 **Opening** (10 minutes)

In advance, prepare bookmarks for the "We Live" activity. These will be placed in students' personal Bibles or in the classroom Bibles used for Sunday School. Cut green construction paper into 2 × 4½-inch strips (or 9 inches long). At the top of the strip, write "OT" on one side and "NT" on the other. Display Posters A, B, and C. Keep these posters on display throughout the quarter. While this lesson does not specifically refer to the map (Poster B), students may enjoy looking at it.

To help familiarize the students with the hymns and catechism songs, play them softly as background music as students gather. Be sure the volume is audible but low, or conversation levels may escalate to compete.

Welcome your students individually as they arrive. Introduce yourself to new students, and make sure the students know one another. As students gather, ask them to draw a picture of the best gift they've ever received.

Begin with the Invocation when all students have gathered. Demonstrate how to make the sign of the cross, touching your forehead, sternum, and each shoulder in turn.

Say In the name of the Father and of the Son and of the Holy Spirit. Amen.

Pray Dear heavenly Father, we thank You for bringing us together for church today, where we can hear Your Word and receive Your forgiveness. Send the Holy Spirit to be with us as we study together. Open our hearts and minds to hear and learn from Your Word. Help us to be thankful for the many blessings You give us each day. In Jesus' name we pray. Amen.

MATERIALS NEEDED

1 Opening
Other Supplies
CD
Posters A, B, and C

2 God Speaks
Teacher Tools
Faith Word Cards 1–2
Poster A
Student Stuff
Bible Discovery Guides
Other Supplies
Rubber bands or paper clips

3 We Live
Teacher Tools
Faith Word Cards 3–4
Poster C (optional)
CD (optional)
Student Stuff
Lesson Leaflets
Bible Discovery Guides
Other Supplies
Construction-paper bookmarks (see Opening)

4 Closing
Teacher Tools
CD
Bible Review Cards 1–8
Other Supplies
Reproducible Page 1 (TG)
Plastic gloves (optional)

Lesson 1

Allow the students a few minutes to tell about the gift they drew. Some students may be uncomfortable speaking to the class, especially if they are new. Ask bolder, more familiar students to share first. Encourage all students to participate, but allow them to pass if they prefer.

Say These are all wonderful gifts and real blessings. Receiving gifts is one way that we know we are loved. Today, we are going to talk about some very wonderful gifts, given to us by God Himself, who loves us very much. Let's sing a hymn of praise and adoration to the Creator of the universe, the God who made us and takes care of us.

Play and sing the hymn "Thy Strong Word" (*LSB* 578; CD 7).

Liturgy Link

Each Divine Service begins with the Invocation and with the sign of the cross as a reminder of our Baptism. It is followed immediately by the Confession and Absolution.

2 God Speaks (20 minutes)

Creation

Give each student a half dozen paper clips or rubber bands. Invite them to shake them in their cupped hands or drop them on a flat surface.

Ask How many of your paper clips (rubber bands) became connected through this accidental impact with one another? (Probably none) **How long do you think you would have to shake them, or how many times would you have to drop them before they would all connect together?** (It probably would never happen.) **What would it take to connect them?** (Careful, thoughtful action) Let them work to connect them together. **Today in our study, we will see that the creation of the world, the miraculous connection of trillions of atoms, did not happen by accident. The Bible tells us how the world was made. It also tells us everything we need to know about God and His plan for our salvation. That plan began at the beginning of the world. Let's read the Bible's account of how the world was created.**

Show the Faith Word Card *create*, and discuss its meaning. The Hebrew word that means "created" is used only when God is the author of the action and only of unique and unprecedented action. On the whiteboard, chalkboard, or large poster paper, draw as large a circle as possible to represent the earth. Have the students open their Bibles to Genesis 1:1.

Explain *Genesis* means "beginning." The Book of Genesis tells the story of the beginning of the world and God's people.

Use Poster A, the Timeline, to indicate that we do not know exactly when the world was created. Ask for volunteer readers, or read the text yourself in the following sections. After each section is read, ask a volunteer to draw the corresponding part of creation on the board or poster paper. (Drawings done on poster paper may be displayed in the classroom or a hallway for students to show to families and friends.) Provide paper and washable markers, and encourage students to create a similar illustration of creation as you work through the study.

From Genesis 1, read verses 1–2 (nothing to draw); verses 3–5 (shade the area surrounding the circle yellow); verses 6–8 (shade top part of circle light blue); verses 9–10 (land at the lower portion of the circle, a body of water); verses 11–13 (plants, trees); verses 14–19 (sun, moon, stars); verses 20–23 (fish, sea creatures, birds); verses 24–25 (animals, reptiles); verses 26–27 (man and woman). Conclude with verses 28–31.

Key Point

God made the world in six days by the power of His Word. All of creation is God's blessing to us.

Lesson 1

Key Point
God made the world in six days by the power of His Word. All of creation is God's blessing to us.

Teacher Tip
Your students' perception of the solar system God created, and their appreciation of God's creative power, might be enhanced by viewing the video "To Scale: the Solar System" (7:07); search for that title on YouTube. Preview the video for suitability for your students and cue it up before class, skipping the ad.

Say **The whole earth was created in just six days by the power of God's Word. Listen as I read chapter 2, verses 1–3.** Confirm that God rested on the seventh day not because He was tired but because He was establishing patterns and priorities for us. He blesses the seventh day and makes it holy, or sets it apart.

Creation vs. Evolution

Distribute the Bible Discovery Guides. Ask the students to write their names on them since you will keep the booklets in the classroom until the end of the quarter. Direct their attention to the Creation chart at the top of page 2. In review, refer to the chart and to the class's drawing, asking what the earth was like before the first day, what God created each day, and so on. Point out that light was created before the sun, moon, and stars. God is able to do far more than our minds can understand.

Refer to the chart in the middle of page 2 of the Bible Discovery Guide, and allow the students to think and ask questions about why evolution is contrary to the Word of God. Christians do not accept evolution because evolution denies that the earth was perfect in its beginning. It also denies that a supreme being—God—made the earth. Evolution claims the earth is moving toward perfection as mutations occur, relying on death—survival of the fittest—for improvements. Scripture tells us that God created the earth to be perfect and that death is a result of sin.

Say **In the First Commandment, God says, "You shall have no other gods." He requires that we believe that He is the only true God, the Creator of the world. God, in Christ, gives us faith to believe that He created the earth and heavens and sustains them by His power and wisdom.**

Draw the students' attention back to the Bible, Genesis 1:26–27.

Say **The first part of verse 26 refers to "our image." What does it mean to be made in God's image? Do we physically look like God?** (No, because God is a spirit. Man was created in God's image with knowledge of God as the source of every blessing [Colossians 3:10]. Man was created in a spiritual likeness of God, in righteousness [Ephesians 4:24].) **Look at Genesis 1:2. Who is present in this verse?** (The Spirit of God) **Now listen while I read John 1:1–5. Whom do these verses speak of?** (The Word is Jesus.) **Was Jesus also present at creation?** (Yes) Review the Bible Words from the back of the Lesson Leaflet, noting that Paul confirms Jesus as the Creator of all things. **What do we call the Father, the Son, and the Holy Spirit together?** (The triune God. Father, Son, and Holy Spirit are the three persons of the Trinity, yet are one God.)

Show the Faith Word Card *triune*. Confirm that the concept of the triune God is impossible for our minds to grasp fully, but that by faith we know it is true.

Ask **Why did God create the world in the order He did?** Allow the students to respond, directing their attention to God's wisdom. Man's dominion shows us that man is the crown of His creation.

Say **The triune God—Father, Son, and Holy Spirit—created the world by His Word. People are the crown of His creation, and He gave humans dominion over the earth. God created the world to be perfect. But as we'll see, it didn't stay perfect. The people God created sinned and fell away from God. But God still loved them.**

Growing in CHRIST

Lesson 1

3 We Live (20 minutes)

With God's Help

Refer to Genesis 1:26, along with verse 28.

Ask **What does it mean to have dominion?** (Caring for, ruling over with love and concern) **If you're in charge of something, how do you treat it?** (Treat it with respect, and take good care of it because you are accountable for it.) **Read verses 29 and 30. What does God say about plants?** (They are for food, for both man and animals.) **God provided for man in His creation, and man was to care for creation.**

Hold a copy of Luther's Small Catechism for students to see (or direct them to the hymnal or Poster C). Ask them to tell what they know about the catechism.

Explain **Martin Luther wrote the Small Catechism more than four hundred years ago to teach ordinary people about God's Word. It summarizes the teachings and language of the Christian faith.** Show the students the First Article.

Say **When we say the Apostles' Creed, we begin by saying, "I believe in God, the Father Almighty, Maker of heaven and earth." We call this the First Article. Listen to what that means.**

Read the explanation, or you may wish to play the catechism songs on the CD (tracks 16–20) and have your students listen for the meaning.

Ask **God still loves us and cares for us. What are some ways God cares for us today?** (He still provides for our needs, such as food, shelter, clothing, education, family, and jobs.) **How should we receive these things?** (With thanksgiving, using them responsibly) **Are we always thankful when we receive the good gifts God provides?** (No, our sinful nature is unappreciative. We complain; we misuse or waste our gifts.) **What are some ways that we can have dominion over the earth? What can we do to take care of it?** (Accept reasonable answers, such as recycling, picking up trash, avoiding products that pollute the earth, not mistreating animals.) Assure the students that though we misuse God's creation and fail to thank Him for His gifts, He still loves us because of the work of His Son. Jesus forgives our sin and brings us new life and salvation through His Holy Word.

Direct the students' attention to page 2 of the Lesson Leaflet. Read the directions. Discuss each picture, and ask students to circle the pictures that illustrate good stewardship of God's creation.

Ask **What is God's response when we don't take care of the earth properly?** (He still forgives our sins, for Jesus' sake.) **God provides our most important gift, and we learn about it in His Word. What is that important gift?** (Jesus, His Son, who died and rose for us) **Through what Jesus did for us, we know that even when we sin and don't do the things we should do, we are forgiven and God still loves us. Does doing good things like taking care of the earth get us to heaven?** (No) **What *does* get us to heaven?** (Faith in Jesus Christ, which is God's gift. We receive the Holy Spirit in our Baptism by the power of God in His Word and in the water. The Means of Grace—God's Word, Baptism, and Holy Communion—provide forgiveness of sins.) **The only way we are**

Lesson 1

Key Point
God made the world in six days by the power of His Word. All of creation is God's blessing to us.

saved is by the grace of God. He gives us faith in His Son, Jesus, who died for our sins and rose again so that we also could live eternally. He comes to us in the Sacraments of Baptism and Holy Communion. Because God loves us, we love others. We do good things because we are *going* to heaven, not to *get* to heaven.

Allow for any questions or comments.

Say **When God created the world, the almighty Word of God was introduced. God's Word is recorded for us in the Bible. Let's take a few minutes today to learn some Bible study skills so that we can become better Bible scholars.**

Show the Faith Word Card *Bible*. Explain that this one book, the Bible, is actually a collection of many books by many authors. Have the students open their Bibles to the table of contents. You may also direct students to page 4 of the Bible Discovery Guide. Point out that the Bible is divided into the Old Testament and the New Testament. Skim through the names of the books, noting that many of them are named for people. Some of these names are the authors; some are the names of the people about or to whom the books were written.

Say **The Bible is the inspired Word of God. That means that even though men wrote the words down on paper, the Holy Spirit gave the men the words to write. Even though many different people did the writing, and the books were written over many years, the Bible never contradicts or disagrees with itself. We understand that the entire Bible *is* the Word of God.**

Have the students turn to the New Testament title page or the first page of Matthew. Distribute the bookmarks you prepared. Explain that *OT* means "Old Testament" and that *NT* means "New Testament." Show them how to insert the bookmark with OT facing the front and NT facing the back. Show the Faith Word Card *testament*.

Say ***Testament* means "covenant with God." A covenant is an agreement. The Old Testament tells about the time before Jesus' birth. That covenant was the promise of the Law that had no power to save people. God knew people couldn't keep the Law perfectly, so He promised a Savior. That promise was given time and again to the people in Old Testament times. The New Testament tells about the time since the Savior's birth. It teaches us about our relationship with God because of Jesus. In both testaments, the "main character" is Jesus.**

Bible Search and Which Gift?

Refer the students to this activity on page 3 of the Lesson Leaflet, and read the directions. Or divide the class into groups and assign specific questions to each group. Have them share answers with the class. The "Which Gift?" activity may be completed at this time also. Read together "Bible Words" on page 4.

Teacher Tip
Pair weaker readers with stronger readers to work on written activities. Be careful not to draw unnecessary attention to the students' varying reading abilities.

Lesson 1

4 Closing (10 minutes)

The First Article

Collect the Bible Discovery Guides and any supplies that will remain in the classroom. Distribute copies of Reproducible Page 1, found at the end of this lesson. Read the First Article together, and compare it to today's Bible Words—Colossians 1:16. Listen to and sing the First Article and Explanation on the CD (CD 16–20). If time permits, allow the students to color the sheet or take it home to color. Encourage them to read it each day as part of the Weekly Devotions found on the Lesson Leaflet. As students color the reproducible page, play the catechism songs on the CD as soft background music. Send students home with the Bible Words Puzzle 1 from the Puzzle Book.

To reinforce the point in "We Live" about taking good care of the gifts God has given us, plan to end class a few minutes early so that students can help clean up the classroom, a room in the church, or perhaps a section of the church property outside. Be careful about keeping students safe from sanitary issues. Provide plastic gloves, for example, if students are picking up litter.

Use Bible Review Cards 1–8 to review the lesson, if you have time. Conclude the lesson with prayer.

Pray Dear heavenly Father, we praise You for the blessing of Your creation and all the blessings You provide every day. Help us be good stewards of Your creation, and forgive us when we aren't. We thank You especially for Your Word, the Bible, through which we learn Your truth; for the Sacraments that assure us of Your forgiveness; and for the faith You give us through Word and Sacrament by the Holy Spirit's power. Be with us this day and forever. We ask all these things in Jesus' name. Amen.

The First Article of the Apostles' Creed

Creation

I believe in God, the Father Almighty, Maker of heaven and earth.

What does this mean? I believe that God has made me and all creatures; that He has given me my body and soul, eyes, ears, and all my members, my reason and all my senses, and still takes care of them.

He also gives me clothing and shoes, food and drink, house and home, wife and children, land, animals, and all I have. He richly and daily provides me with all that I need to support this body and life.

He defends me against all danger and guards and protects me from all evil. All this He does only out of fatherly, divine goodness and mercy, without any merit or worthiness in me. For all this it is my duty to thank and praise, serve and obey Him.

This is most certainly true.

UPPER ELEMENTARY

Preparing the Lesson

God Creates Adam and Eve
Genesis 1:26–2:25

Lesson 2

_____
Date of Use

Key Point
God has made us in His image, provides all things for our good, and makes us rulers over the earth and everything in it.

Law/**Gospel**
God appoints me as a caretaker of His creation and expects me to take care of it for His glory and the good of others. **God provides me with all good things for this life and forgives me for Jesus' sake when I put myself above Him and His creation or when I misuse or neglect my vocation to rule the earth properly.**

Context
Some have argued that Genesis 2 is a second account of creation. But Genesis 2 presupposes the five preceding days of creation. This chapter reviews in more detail the creation of mankind in Adam and Eve.

Commentary
The name *Adam* means "earth" and points to humanity's material aspect. But the "breath," or "spirit," of God makes Adam a living being and gives him fellowship with God. God is the source of life—turning away from that source leads to death. Having God's Spirit in Genesis 2 corresponds to being made in the image of God in Genesis 1. The earthly blessings that follow express the love God has for Adam.

Eden is sometimes called "Paradise" (garden). The tree of life within Eden may have been planted near running or "living" water—as in Psalm 1:3. Note that the tree of life and living water are linked again in Revelation 22:1–2.

The tree of the knowledge of good and evil is sometimes identified as an apple tree because the Latin words for *evil* and *apple* share the same root, *mal*. Jewish tradition pictures the tree of the knowledge of good and evil as a citron tree or a grapevine. But the actual fruit is never identified in Scripture.

Four rivers flow from around Eden, including two that were the mainstay of Mesopotamian life and civilization: the Tigris and the Euphrates. The locations of the other two rivers have not been identified, perhaps due to changes to the earth's surface during the worldwide flood later in Genesis.

Man is given the task of working the garden. To this day, work, or vocation, remains one of our innate needs. Adam's naming of the animals shows mastery as well as intelligence.

Note the underlying pattern, hierarchy, and priority. There are things above and below; all things are good, but some are better—or could be better. Adam in Paradise needs a "suitable helper." The woman is created from his flesh so that he will care for her as for himself. Moses issues a command: "Therefore a man shall leave his father and his mother and hold fast to his wife, and they shall become one flesh" (Genesis 2:24). The marriage relationship has priority even over parental obligations.

The man and woman were naked and without shame. They were open and trusting, with nothing to hide. A child with beautiful freckles may be made ashamed due to hurtful comments and insults and then may internalize that shame. Shame arises from evil without as well as from evil within; Paradise was free of both. Living according to God's Law brings earthly blessing. The man Adam foreshadows Christ, the new Adam (Romans 5:12–21), who brings believers into eternal paradise (Luke 23:43).

To hear an in-depth discussion of this Bible account, visit cph.org/podcast and listen to our Seeds of Faith podcast each week.

Lesson 2

God Creates Adam and Eve

Genesis 1:26–2:25

Connections

Bible Words
I praise You, for I am fearfully and wonderfully made. Psalm 139:14 (CD 8)

Faith Words
image of God, dominion, inspiration, translation

Hymn
From All That Dwell Below the Skies (*LSB* 816; CD 1)

Catechism
Apostles' Creed: First Article (CD 16–20)

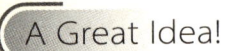

1 Opening (5 minutes)

In advance, prepare bookmarks for the "We Live" activity. These will be placed in the students' personal Bibles or in the classroom Bibles used for Sunday School. Cut red and blue construction paper into 2 × 4½-inch strips (or 9 inches long). For each student, prepare five red bookmarks with these five different labels: *Books of Moses*, *History*, *Poetry*, *Major Prophets*, *Minor Prophets*. Prepare three blue bookmarks for each student labeled *Gospels/History*, *Epistles*, and *Prophecy* for the Lesson Leaflet activity.

For "God Speaks," cover a table with white paper, newsprint, or a paper tablecloth. Have available markers or crayons and several 4 × 11-inch pieces of paper that have been folded in half crosswise to make paper tents. As students arrive, give them a ball of play dough to shape. (Check children's activity books or the Internet for an inexpensive play dough recipe. Provide plastic zipper bags if the play dough will be taken home.) Ask them to create a living creature.

Begin with the Invocation. Make the sign of the cross.

Say In the name of the Father and of the Son and of the Holy Spirit. Amen.

Sing "From All That Dwell Below the Skies" (*LSB* 816; CD 1), reminding students of our worship of the triune God.

Pray Dear heavenly Father, thank You for bringing us to church today to hear Your Word and to see You in Your Sacraments. Thank You for creating all things, including us, and for caring for us every day. Thank You that

MATERIALS NEEDED

1 Opening	2 God Speaks	3 We Live	4 Closing
Teacher Tools CD **Other Supplies** Play dough Zipper bags (optional)	**Teacher Tools** Posters A and B **Student Stuff** Bible Discovery Guide Lesson Leaflets **Other Supplies** Newsprint or paper tablecloth Play dough Resource Page 2 (TG; optional)	**Teacher Tools** Faith Word Cards 5–8 CD **Student Stuff** Lesson Leaflets Bible Discovery Guide **Other Supplies** Construction-paper bookmarks (see Opening)	**Teacher Tools** CD Bible Review Cards 1–16 **Student Stuff** Bible Discovery Guide **Other Supplies** Reproducible Page 2 (TG)

through Your Son, Jesus, You are re-creating us in Your image. In heaven, that image will be fully restored in us. Be with us now as we study Your Word. In Jesus' name we pray. Amen.

2 God Speaks (15 minutes)

Ask the students to show their play dough creations to the class.

Say **I asked you to create a living creature. These look like living things, but I notice that none of them are alive yet. Breathe life into your creations, and make them come alive.** The students will realize they cannot. **Can anyone make his or her creation come to life?** Direct the students as necessary to arrive at the conclusion that only God can create life.

Use the Bible Discovery Guide charts to help review the events of creation. Have a few extra copies of Reproducible Page 1, "The First Article," on hand for students who may not have received one. Post one in your classroom for reference throughout the quarter. Ask the students to summarize the story of creation: God created the earth and everything in it in six days and rested from His work on the seventh day. Review the First Article and explanation in Luther's Small Catechism (also found on Resource Page 2 in the back of this guide or on the CD). Remind them that God not only created the world and everything in it, including people, but He also takes care of it all.

Say **Today's story is a close-up of what happened on the sixth day of creation, when God created man and woman.**

Adam and Eve in the Garden

Display Poster B. Point out the Tigris (TIE gris) and Euphrates (you FRAY tease) Rivers, and tell students that Bible scholars believe the Garden of Eden was located between them. Note also on Poster A that we cannot assign a specific date to this lesson.

Say **We are going to create a model of the Garden of Eden where God placed His people.**

Assign students to make Adam, Eve, and animals out of their play dough. Assign other students to draw the river that divides into four rivers, the aquatic life, and the green vegetation on the paper-covered table. (Pencil in a rough outline to guide the students in creating the Garden of Eden on the paper-covered table, using the entire table for the model.) Assign one or two others to draw trees and plants for food, and one or two others to draw the tree of the knowledge of good and evil and the tree of life on the outside of the folded paper tents. These tents will be set up on the tabletop drawing for a 3-D effect. Position the students around the table, and indicate in which area they are to add their creations.

Say **As I read, listen and then create your part.** Read the story text from Genesis 1:26–2:25 as the students work quietly to create their portion of the model. **Now, let's use the things we've created to retell the story.** Demonstrate how to set up the paper trees; identify the garden and ask for volunteers to retell how things were created in today's reading.

Key Point

God has made us in His image, provides all things for our good, and makes us rulers over the earth and everything in it.

Teacher Tip

Extremely active students may have difficulty with self-control during this creation activity. As an alternative activity, you may choose to have the students complete the drawing on page 2 of the Lesson Leaflet as you read.

Lesson 2

Key Point

God made us in His image, provides all things for our good, and makes us rulers over the earth and everything in it.

3 We Live (20 minutes)

Show the Faith Word Card *image of God*.

Say **In Genesis 1:26, we read that the triune God created people in His image. What does it mean to be created in the image of God?** (In a spiritual likeness of God, in righteousness, having knowledge of God as the source of every blessing, being without sin so that we perfectly know and gladly do His will) **How is man created differently from the animals and other living things?** (The rest of creation came into existence through the Word of God. God was more deliberate when He created man. He formed man out of the dust of the earth and breathed life into him. People are the crown of creation, the special focus of God's love. All of creation was brought into existence to serve man. God made the habitat for His children to live in. [Compare this to parents who provide a place for their family to live. They do it because of their love for the family.])

Review the Bible Words (Psalm 139:14) from the back of the Lesson Leaflet. Challenge your students to commit the verse to memory. Or listen to and then sing the recording of this Bible verse using your teacher CD, track 8.

Ask **How did God provide a helper for Adam?** (No suitable helper was found among the animals, so God caused Adam to fall into a deep sleep and created woman out of his rib. Eve was created as a helper for Adam. God brought Adam and Eve together as husband and wife, creating marriage as a blessing for them and all their descendants.) **What was the special task God gave to Adam?** (To have dominion over the rest of creation, to care for the garden)

Show the Faith Word Card *dominion*, and discuss the meaning. Notice that God gave Adam the task of caring for the garden before the fall into sin. Being able to care for God's creation was intended to be a blessing for Adam, not a chore.

Ask **What did God provide for Adam and Eve in the Garden of Eden?** (Everything they needed. Plants were given for food.) **What restrictions did God give about the food?** (They could eat of any of the trees except for the tree of the knowledge of good and evil.) **Why did God put the tree of the knowledge of good and evil in the garden if He didn't want Adam and Eve to eat the fruit?** (God created people in holiness. He gave them free will to obey and to maintain that holiness by choice. Because people had free will, their obedience to God was a loving response to His blessings.) **Do we still have dominion over all of God's creation today?** (Yes. God gave us the responsibility to take care of the earth, respect creation, and use its resources wisely for the glory of God and the good of others. This is being a good steward of what God has given us. We must be careful not to view the creation to be more important than other people or the Creator. Creation is still provided by God for the benefit of mankind.) **Do we always make good choices about how we care for creation?** (Because of our sinful nature, we cannot always make the right choices. Sometimes, we are wasteful of resources.) **God, in Christ, offers us forgiveness when we exploit, waste, or spoil His creation, and He continues in mercy to grant all that we need in body and spirit.**

Say **Some people make a religion out of worshiping creation. They believe that people are only a small part of the earth and that the earth is more important than people. This is not what the Bible teaches. Having dominion over creation is not the same as worshiping it. We sin when we worship the**

18 Growing in CHRIST.

creation and not the Creator. Jesus forgives our sins of idolatry when we place the creation higher than God. God deserves our worship and praise.

Conclude People were made without sin and were given a chance to maintain that perfect condition. But that didn't happen. People sinned by disobeying God. Yet God's love for His creation was so great that He provided a way to save people from their sin. As we read in the First Article of the Apostles' Creed, God still provides everything we need for life on this earth. He also provides the way that we can be forgiven for all our sins. **How did He do this?** (He sent His Son, Jesus Christ, to die for us and rise again.) **Because of what Jesus did for us, we will be re-created in the image of God when we get to heaven. Through our Baptism, we are washed clean from our sins, and through Jesus, God sees us without sin. We are made holy again and righteous. When we are in heaven, we will once again be in the image of God.** See Ephesians 4:24 and Romans 5:18–19.

Bible Study Skills

Say **In Lesson 1, we began to learn some Bible study skills.** Review the concepts of the Old and New Testaments. **Here are two more words that we use when we talk about our Bibles.**

Show the Faith Word Cards *inspiration* and *translation*. Discuss the meanings and other forms of *inspiration*, such as *inspire* and *inspired*.

Say **Today, we're going to see how each testament is divided and learn how to find Bible passages.**

Direct the students' attention to the Bible bookcase on page 4 of the Bible Discovery Guide, which illustrates the divisions of the Old and New Testaments. Look briefly over the list, and use the following descriptions to discuss the characteristics of each set of books. Review the books in each division by name.

Books of Moses: early history of God's people, written by Moses

History: additional history after Moses' death

Poetry: writings that show the wisdom of God

Prophets: God's message to His people through men

Gospels: descriptions of the life and work of Jesus

Acts: a historical account of the disciples' work to spread the Gospel

Epistles: letters to early Christians that teach how to understand Scripture

Prophecy: the vision to John, things that have not all happened yet

Work together as a class to insert the bookmarks correctly. Cite page numbers if possible, and assist students individually as necessary. These will become useful tools for future use. Using the table of contents, have the students open their Bibles to the first page of Genesis and insert the red "Books of Moses" bookmark. Open to Joshua and insert the "History" bookmark. Continue in the same way for "Poetry," beginning with Job; "Major Prophets," beginning with Isaiah; and "Minor Prophets," beginning with Hosea. Move into the New Testament to insert the blue bookmarks. The "Gospels/History" section begins with Matthew. The "Epistles" begin with Romans. Revelation is the only New Testament book to follow the "Prophecy" bookmark. These markers will remain in the students' Bibles as ongoing aids. You may refer to the bookmarks as reference points when asking students to find passages, for example, "Jeremiah is a prophetic book."

Lesson 2

Key Point

God made us in His image, provided all things for our good, and made us rulers over the earth and everything in it.

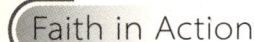

Find It in Scripture

Direct students to page 3 of the Lesson Leaflet. Ask for volunteers to read the text. Demonstrate to the students where to find the book names, chapter numbers, and verse numbers. Point out that most Bibles have references listed in the upper outside corners. These are used like guide words in a dictionary. The verse listed in the upper left corner is the first verse found on that two-page spread; the upper right corner has the last verse found on the two-page spread. Work through the "Bible Reference" exercises.

4 Closing (10 minutes)

Encourage memorization of the Bible books by having the children practice the reading of the names from the Bible Discovery Guide page. Spend a little time during each lesson reciting them. Make copies of Bible Words Puzzle 2 for students to complete at home.

Review the First Article using the catechism songs on the CD. Use the Bible Review Cards from this lesson and Lesson 1 to play one of the Bible Review Games in the "Resource Pages" section of this Teacher Guide.

Read aloud the hymn "On My Heart Imprint Your Image" (*LSB* 422) below as a prayer. If you have hymnals, the students could read the first two lines and the teacher can read the last two for emphasis and explanation. Or you could sing the hymn together. Consider coordinating ahead and leading the students to the adult Bible classroom to sing the song for them. Return to your classroom for parent pickup. Pray the following prayer before dismissal.

Pray **Dear heavenly Father, we thank and praise You that You have created us and that You continue to provide everything we need. Be with us now as we leave Your house and begin another week in Your care. In Jesus' name we pray. Amen.**

The Creation Word Search on Reproducible Page 2, found at the end of this lesson, can be used to fill extra moments at the end of class or can be a take-home activity. Have a copy available for each of your students.

On My Heart Imprint Your Image

On my heart imprint Your image, Blessed Jesus, King of grace,

That life's riches, cares, and pleasures Never may Your work erase;

Let the clear inscription be: Jesus, crucified for me,

Is my life, my hope's foundation, And my glory and salvation!

LSB 422

Growing in CHRIST

Creation Word Search

Adam	stars	dominion	creation	night
triune	plants	light	day	image of God
Eve	seas	moon	heavens	earth
Word	creatures	fish	birds	garden

```
D S N E V A E H C W
O O M U S E A S K D
M A L Y V A X B R B
I C R E A T I O N I
N I G H T M W U M R
I M A G E O F G O D
O E D O U I T A O S
N B A J S D H R N M
E I M H S Y T D R O
P N G D A T R E V R
D A Y H P L A N T S
S E R U T A E R C A
G T R I U N E T S S
F O G S Z L I G H T
```

UPPER ELEMENTARY

Preparing the Lesson

Sin Enters the World
Genesis 3

Lesson 3

_____
Date of Use

Key Point
Through Adam, sin spreads to all people. Through Christ, God offers forgiveness to all people.

Law/**Gospel**
Because I sin, I will die. **God sent His Son, Jesus, to crush sin, death, and the devil, and through Him, God forgives my sins and gives me eternal life.**

Context
It appears that angels were created before the earth and that some rebelled during that time (Job 38:4–7; 2 Peter 2:4). St. Augustine reasoned that the fall of some angels must have occurred at the instant of their creation, when they chose to look to self instead of to God; otherwise, they would have known that God's service is infinitely sweeter than self-service. We say that those angels who know the sweetness of serving God are confirmed in grace and will never fall away.

Evil is not part of the created world; it arises from disordered love. In Eve's case, she placed the love of knowledge (a good thing) over obedience (a better thing).

Commentary
The serpent, or snake, is identified as Satan ("accuser") in Revelation 12:9. He is "crafty," which implies manipulation to suit self, as opposed to being wise, which implies conforming self to God's truth. The serpent begins with an implied lie: "Did God actually say . . . ?" (Genesis 3:1). He attacks Eve's faith, her confidence in what God had said. He continues with a bald-faced lie: "You will not surely die. . . . Your eyes will be opened, and you will be like God" (vv. 4–5).

Eve chooses to believe the serpent rather than God. Sin is breaking the Law (1 John 3:4) or disobeying God, but its roots lie in the lack of faith in what God has said. Characteristically, Satan leads us from doubt of God's Law into sin; then he leads us, in our guilt, to doubt God's Gospel and to despair.

Adam trusts his wife more than God's Word, and so he follows her into sin. Now they "know" (experience) the difference between good and evil. Feeling self-conscious and ashamed, they cover themselves. The sound of God walking in the cool of the day is no longer welcome but is a cause of dread. Confronted with guilt, Adam blames God and Eve: "the woman whom You gave to be with me" (Genesis 3:12). Eve blames the serpent.

God's curse of the serpent is good news for the descendants of Adam. Genesis 3:15 is known as the protoevangel, or "first Gospel." The woman's Seed would be victorious, crushing the head of the serpent despite being wounded in the process. The tree of the knowledge of good and evil became the instrument of condemnation; the tree of the cross would become the instrument of salvation.

God's judgment on Eve takes the form of a "cross" laid on marriage. Now this gift will entail the pain of childbearing, and the husband's rule will be experienced as oppression. The judgment on Adam is the frustration and drudgery of work, ending in the return to dust through physical death.

God makes garments of skins for Adam and Eve (v. 21); animals had to die. Thereafter, human life, both physical and spiritual, is sustained by the death or sacrifice of animals. The closing judgment against both Adam and Eve is for them to be driven from Eden with its tree of (eternal) life. What they were made for is closed off to them and their descendants. Mankind has lost the image of God until it is restored in Christ, the new Adam.

To hear an in-depth discussion of this Bible account, visit cph.org/podcast and listen to our Seeds of Faith podcast each week.

Lesson 3

Sin Enters the World

Genesis 3

Connections

Bible Words
For our sake [God] made Him to be sin who knew no sin, so that in Him we might become the righteousness of God. 2 Corinthians 5:21 (CD 13)

Faith Words
original sin, enmity, sin, righteous

Hymn
The Tree of Life (*LSB* 561; CD 6)

Catechism
Apostles' Creed: Second Article

Liturgy
Confession of Sins

1 Opening (5 minutes)

Play the First Article and Explanation catechism songs from the CD (tracks 16–20) as background music while students arrive.

Prior to the arrival of the students, write the Faith Words for this lesson (original sin, enmity, sin, righteous) and the following sentences on the chalkboard, whiteboard, or a large piece of paper.

1. An attitude of being enemies is _____.
2. When I "miss the mark," I _____.
3. Every person born since Adam and Eve sinned has _____.
4. Being free from guilt or sin is being _____.

Allow students to complete the sentences by writing the correct word in the blanks, or let them attach the Faith Word Card to the board or paper. Keep the sentences visible throughout the lesson for easy reference.

Write headings on the chalkboard or whiteboard for one or more simple topics: for example, favorite flavors of ice cream or favorite snack. As students arrive, greet them individually and have them each vote with a tally mark under the heading of their choice. Add headings as necessary, and vote your own choice also. As you look at the results, stress that each one in the class is created as a unique individual, yet there are many things you have in common.

Begin with the Invocation. Invite the children to make the sign of the cross to remind them of their Baptism.

Say In the name of the Father and of the Son and of the Holy Spirit. Amen.

MATERIALS NEEDED

1 Opening	2 God Speaks	3 We Live	4 Closing
Teacher Tools Faith Word Cards 9–12 CD	**Teacher Tools** Lesson Leaflets Poster D **Other Supplies** Construction paper in purple, red, and green (optional)	**Teacher Tools** Faith Word Cards 3–5, 7, 9–12 CD **Student Stuff** Bible Discovery Guides Lesson Leaflets **Other Supplies** Reproducible Page 3 (TG) Resource Page 2 (TG; optional)	**Teacher Tools** Bible Review Cards 1–24 CD Poster D **Other Supplies** Resource Pages 6–8

Lesson 3

Pray Dear heavenly Father, thank You for creating us and giving us all good things. We know that we are sinful, and we ask You to forgive us when we sin. Thank You for sending Your Son, Jesus, to be our Savior. Bless us as we learn in Sunday School today. In His name we pray. Amen.

Doing the Right Thing

Get your students up on their feet to play "Simon Says."

Explain When I say, "Simon says (*name an action*)," you do it. But when I just say, "(*name an action*)," don't do it. Play for a couple of minutes. When playing this game, it's not important who wins or loses. Allow all children to continue playing, even if they make mistakes. **Even when we know exactly what we should do, we aren't always able to do it. That's what sin is: we know what is right and wrong, but we don't always do the right thing. Sin is disobeying God. Today, our story is about Adam and Eve's first sin, and what God did for them—and for us—to make everything right again.**

Have the students return to their seats.

2 God Speaks (10 minutes)

Ask for volunteer readers, or have the students follow along as you read the story from the Lesson Leaflet. With a pencil or crayon, ask the students to underline the parts of the story that show the sin Adam and Eve committed. Underlined items should include Eve's doubting God's Word, eating the fruit, sharing the fruit, hiding from God, and blaming each other. Circle (or underline with a different color) the consequences of sin, including God's curse on the serpent, pain in bearing children, working for a living, and being sent from the Garden of Eden. Draw a box around (or underline with a third color) the words that show God still cares for them. Include God calling to Adam and Eve, wanting them to confess, clothing them, and promising a Savior.

Or give each student three squares of colored construction paper: purple for sin, red for consequence, and green for God's care. Have them hold up the appropriate square when they see that kind of action in the text. (You can simplify this activity by helping students mark the eating of the fruit as sin, being sent out of the garden as consequence, and the promise of the Savior as God's care.)

Point out that the hymn on Poster D traces the events of the Bible account quite closely.

3 We Live (25 minutes)

Say Adam and Eve disobeyed God. Satan caused Eve to doubt that she would die. He wanted Eve to believe that God was withholding special blessings and knowledge. Eve ate the fruit and gave some to Adam, and he ate too. This first act of disobedience brought sin into the world. Adam and Eve no longer reflected the image of God. From that point on, every person born has been sinful. This is what we call *original sin*. Show the Faith Word Card, and discuss the meaning.

Key Point
Through Adam, sin spreads to all people. Through Christ, God offers forgiveness to all people.

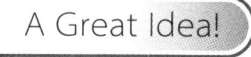
A Great Idea!

Liturgy Link
Man's image is one of sinfulness rather than of perfect holiness. In the Confession of Sins in the Divine Service, we state that we are "by nature sinful and unclean." Our natural state has been corrupted by sin. We are born as enemies of God, doing that which is contrary to His will.

Lesson 3

We, too, are sinners. We don't obey God and His Word. We blame others for our sins. We try to be like God. Because we are sinners, we deserve punishment and death. God didn't abandon Adam and Eve. He hasn't abandoned us. He had a different plan to make things right again. Have students turn to Genesis 3:14–15, and read the verses to them. Show the Faith Word Cards *enmity* and *sin,* and discuss the meanings. **Sin makes us enemies of God.**

Ask **Who is the "He" in verse 15?** Have students turn to John 3:16 and read the verse aloud. Make the connection between the "He" of Genesis 3:15 and Jesus.

Say **Right from the time sin entered into the world, God knew what He would do to someday restore people to His image. He would send Jesus to do for people what people couldn't do on their own. Jesus came to crush sin, death, and the devil by dying on the cross and rising again.**

Turn to page 4 of the Lesson Leaflet, and read the Bible Words together. Review the definition of *image of God* (5), and introduce the Faith Word Card *righteous*. Discuss how "without sin" is the same as being righteous—we are right with God, just as when He created us in His image. Christ made us right with God by His perfect life, suffering, and death.

Play and sing the Bible Words song found on the CD, track 13.

Say **As soon as sin came into the world, God planned for the Savior to make things right again. He sent His Son, Jesus Christ, so that those who believe in Him would inherit eternal life. Jesus makes us righteous because He died for our sins and rose from the dead. Listen to Romans 6:4.** Read the verse. **How does this righteousness come to us?** (Through Baptism, our sins are washed away. We live a new life in Christ.) Read Revelation 2:7. **Where will we have a chance to eat from the tree of life?** (In heaven. Because of Jesus' death and resurrection, we will be fully restored to the image of God when we get to heaven.) Read the Second Article and its explanation in the Small Catechism or from Resource Page 2 in the back of this guide. (You may wish to provide copies for your students' use in class.) Allow for sharing of what this means to each of the students before moving into the Bible Study Skills portion of the lesson.

Key Point
Through Adam, sin spreads to all people. Through Christ, God offers forgiveness to all people.

Bible Study Skills

Ask student volunteers to tell you what they have learned so far in their Bible study skills practice. Direct their answers as necessary to include Faith Word Cards for *Bible* and *testament* (3 and 4), divisions in books including Old and New Testaments, sections that correspond to the bookmarks placed in their Bibles, how to read a reference, and so on. If time permits, read "God's Word in Print" together from the Bible Discovery Guide. Emphasize that the Scriptures are the inspired Word of God; the words were written on paper by many different authors over a long period of time, but God Himself inspired the words. Because God is perfect and does not lie, Scripture does not contradict itself.

Say **Today, we're going to learn about studying the Bible on our own. Open your Bibles to 2 Timothy 3:16–17.** Assist by pointing out that this is in the New Testament, in the Epistles section.

Students may pair up to look up Bible verses for this section of the activity. Another option is to print the texts in advance of the lesson as mini posters on 8½ × 11-inch paper.

Ask What does this verse tell us about God's Word? (All Scripture comes from God directly. Show Faith Word Card 7, *inspiration*. We can learn many things from Scripture so that we can be equipped to live God-pleasing lives.) Show the Faith Word Card *righteous* again.

Remind What we do doesn't get us to heaven. What Jesus did for us gets us to heaven. By studying God's Word, we can know Jesus better. We can be equipped to love others when we understand how God loves us. Ask students to turn to Colossians 3:16.

Ask When the Word of God "dwells" in us, it lives there; it's present all the time. How does this happen? (Through attending the church service, where God's Word is preached, and through our study of God's Word) Turn to Romans 10:17. **What happens when we hear the Word of God?** (The Holy Spirit creates faith in us.)

Encourage your students in their personal Bible study; suggest "Weekly Devotions" using the Bible readings and other resources on page 4 of the leaflet.

God's Word For Me

Distribute copies of Reproducible Page 3, found at the end of this lesson. Read the first paragraph. Assist the students in writing a simple prayer and answering the questions. Stress that reading the Bible isn't a requirement for our salvation, but when we read and study God's Word, God works in our lives, equipping us to serve Him by serving others. Encourage the students to take the chart home and to fill it in as they read the Bible each day, sharing this learning with family. Encourage the students to regularly attend the worship services at your church. Here, too, they will hear God's Word.

Make copies of Bible Words Puzzle 3 for students to complete at home.

4 Closing (10 minutes)

Practice reciting the Bible Books to aid in the students' memorization of them. Allow five minutes or so to play one of the Bible Review Games (Resource Pages 6–8), including the questions from the Bible Review Cards for today's lesson and previous ones.

Have students look at the hymn "The Tree of Life" (*LSB* 561; CD 6). You can make copies of the lyrics or melody-line score from the files on the CD or have the students follow the words on Poster D. Point out in the first stanza that God allowed the man and woman to eat from the tree of life but not from another tree in the garden. Point out that in stanzas 3 and 4, the tree of life is the cross of Christ. Before sin, Adam and Eve were created in the image of God and had a right relationship with Him. Read again Revelation 2:7. The tree of life is in heaven. When we go to heaven, because of what Christ has done for us, we will be restored to the image of God and will also eat of the tree of life. Sing the hymn. Close with prayer.

Pray Dear heavenly Father, we thank You for Your plan of salvation, that You sent Your Son, Jesus, to die for our sins and to rise again. Forgive our sins when we do wrong, and send Your Holy Spirit to help us understand Your precious Word. We pray in Jesus' name. Amen.

God's Word for Me

Studying the Bible on your own can be a very special time between you and God. He promises to bless us when we read the Bible. The Holy Spirit will help us understand the Bible. He gives us faith at our Baptism to believe in Jesus. Before you read and study the Bible, ask the Holy Spirit to give you understanding. Ask Him to make you really want to read God's Word every day. Pray also that Jesus Christ, who dwells in you, will strengthen your faith in Him. When you read the Bible, you may have questions about some things. Ask your pastor to help you understand.

Write your prayer here.

_____
_____
_____
_____.

Make a plan for studying the Bible on your own this week. Here are some ideas:

A good place would be _____.

A good time would be _____.

Before I read, I want to remember to _____.

I could read _____.

After reading, write one sentence about what you learned.

_____.

Bible Study Chart

Date	Passage	What I Learned

UPPER ELEMENTARY

Preparing the Lesson

Cain and Abel

Genesis 4:1–16

Lesson 4

Date of Use

Key Point

Even though Cain sinned, God still loved and preserved him. Even though we sin, God, in Christ, still loves and preserves us.

Law/**Gospel**

I sin when I trust myself or my own deeds to please God. **God loves me and sent His Son, Jesus, to be the perfect sacrifice for my sin. Through faith in Him, I am marked as God's child and receive His gifts of forgiveness, life, and salvation.**

Context

The biblical chapter divisions with which we are familiar were not added until the completed Scriptures were already one thousand years old. Neither they nor the chapter headings added by modern editors are part of the inspired Word. Genesis 4 is often designated as being about Cain and Abel. The chapter is really about Adam, now cursed by sin.

Adam and Eve did not physically die the same day they first sinned; they lived on, raised children, had hopes dashed, and experienced the death of one child at the hand of another.

Commentary

Eve's words in Genesis 4:1 could be translated "I have brought forth a man, the Lord." Some scholars have seen this as her expectation that Cain was the one to crush the serpent. If so, these hopes would be dashed.

The offering made by Abel, the shepherd, proved acceptable to God, while that of Cain, the farmer, did not. Hebrews 11:4 states that Abel made the acceptable offering by faith. Cain's feelings of disappointment and jealousy boiled over into a premeditated act of murder. Ironically, his desire to please God on one level led to this sinful impulse.

Abel, the innocent shepherd whose offering was accepted by God, was killed for it. In this way, Abel was a type (foreshadowing) of Christ. Abel is the first example of the persecution of the faithful—what St. Augustine called the war waged by the city of man on the city of God.

God confronts Cain, who responds with a lie, followed by this impudent question: "Am I my brother's keeper?" (Genesis 4:9). The implied answer is yes.

As Adam was cursed for his sin, so Cain is also cursed; however, the mark of Cain is actually a sign of mercy proclaiming an end to vengeance. Like other laws of God, it protects people from the coarse outbursts of sin. Cain's line of descendants does not produce the promised Seed—that comes through Seth, who is born later—and, after a brief genealogy, Scripture tells us no more about Cain.

To hear an in-depth discussion of this Bible account, visit cph.org/podcast and listen to our Seeds of Faith podcast each week.

Lesson 4

Cain and Abel

Genesis 4:1–16

Connections

Bible Words
The Lord . . . is patient toward you, not wishing that any should perish, but that all should reach repentance. 2 Peter 3:9 (CD 15)

Faith Words
worship, repentance, preserves, perish

Hymn
From All That Dwell Below the Skies (*LSB* 816; CD 1)

Catechism
Apostles' Creed: Third Article
First Commandment
Fifth Commandment

1 Opening (5 minutes)

Scramble the spelling of the Faith Words for today's lesson on the chalkboard or large paper for the children to unscramble as they arrive. Provide enough blanks underneath each word so the letters can be written in the correct order. Give clues by filling in one or two letters of each word. Scrambled spelling: *pshwroi, panentrece, psreevsre, pishre*. You will be able to refer to them along with the use of the Faith Word Cards throughout the lesson.

Begin with the Invocation when all of the students have gathered. Make the sign of the cross.

Say In the name of the Father and of the Son and of the Holy Spirit. Amen.

Pray Dear heavenly Father, no matter how hard we may try to hide the truth, You still know what is in our hearts. Thank You for Your Word, the Law and Gospel, which convicts us of sin and tells us of forgiveness through your Son, Jesus. Be with us as we study Your Word today. In Jesus' name we pray. Amen.

Play and sing "From All That Dwell Below the Skies" (*LSB* 816; CD 1).

MATERIALS NEEDED

1 Opening	2 God Speaks	3 We Live	4 Closing
Teacher Tools CD	**Teacher Tools** Faith Word Cards 13–15 **Student Stuff** Bible Discovery Guide **Other Supplies** Button or small object to hide Adhesive notes	**Teacher Tools** Faith Word Cards 14–16; CD **Student Stuff** Lesson Leaflets **Other Supplies** Reproducible Page 4 (TG) Slips of paper, container Bookmarks as prizes (optional) Resource Page 2 (TG; optional)	**Teacher Tools** Bible Review Cards 1–32 CD **Other Supplies** Resource Pages 6–8 (TG; optional)

Lesson 4

② God Speaks (18 minutes)

Play a game of "Who's Got the Button?" as students gather. One student, the guesser, hides eyes or leaves the room as others decide who will conceal in their possession a button or similar object. Students stand in a line holding their closed fists straight out in front of them in one long line. One fist contains the button. The guesser studies the faces of his or her classmates and tries to determine who is concealing the button by their responses to questions, facial expressions, and body language. The guesser chooses the fists one at a time. The student opens the chosen fist. If that fist was empty, it is removed from the line by placing it behind the student's back. The guesser keeps guessing until the button is found. When a person is caught with the button, he or she becomes the next guesser.

Relate the game of "Who's Got the Button?" to today's story.

Say Sometimes, we can tell who is telling us the truth; sometimes, it's harder to determine. But God always knows the truth, no matter how we try to hide it. In today's story, Cain tried to cover up his sins of unacceptable worship and of murder. But God knew the truth.

Open Bibles to Genesis 4, and ask for volunteers to read today's story in the following segments. Follow each segment with the questions that relate. Begin with verses 1–5.

Ask Who were the first two sons of Adam and Eve? What were their occupations? (Cain worked the ground and grew crops, and Abel tended sheep.) **These passages record an act of worship. How did the brothers worship in the Bible account?** Use the Faith Word Card *worship* to explain worship. (They each gave an offering from their products.) **What problem did the brothers have in this story?** (They each brought an offering, but God accepted only Abel's offering.) **Read Hebrews 11:4. Why did God accept Abel's offering but not Cain's offering?** (Not because of the offering itself, but because Abel made his offering in faith, knowing that he was an unworthy sinner needing God's gift of forgiveness, life, and salvation. He believed that God is gracious and full of compassion. Cain's sacrifice lacked faith. God looked at the person rather than the work of the sacrifice. Nothing, including worship, is pleasing to God unless it is done in faith. See Romans 14:23b and Proverbs 15:8–9.) **How did Cain's reaction make matters worse?** (He became angry.)

Ask for volunteers to read verses 6–7.

Say God is being loving in these verses. What is He trying to get Cain to understand? (Because Cain lacked faith in God, his sacrifice was unacceptable to God. Perhaps Cain was relying on the fact that he was the firstborn son of Adam and Eve and more worthy because of it. By relying on himself, Cain was saying he didn't need God. He must love God with all his heart, mind, and soul. [See Matthew 22:37–38.] Sin is so big that it can only be removed by God's mercy, which must be accepted by faith. God wanted Cain to know and believe that the Savior promised to his parents and him was the person he needed to look to for forgiveness and salvation. Abel relied on God's grace and mercy, and his sacrifice was accepted.)

Key Point
Even though Cain sinned, God still loved and preserved him. Even though we sin, God, in Christ, still loves and preserves us.

A Great Idea!

Teacher Tip
Scripture interprets itself; that is, we understand the meaning of God's Word from what other passages of Scripture tell us. Use Genesis 4:5 and Hebrews 11:4 as an example of Scripture interpreting itself.

Lesson 4

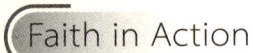

Key Point
Even though Cain sinned, God still loved and preserved him. Even though we sin, God, in Christ, still loves and preserves us.

Ask students to turn to page 6 in their Bible Discovery Guide to see how work changed after sin entered into the world. Encourage students to think of adults they know who work very hard. How can they help that person this week? Record answers from each student on adhesive notes. Encourage the students to take the note home as a reminder to help in the days to come.

Read verses 8–12.

Say Cain's anger caused him to kill his brother. Even though Cain didn't answer God's question truthfully, God knew what had happened. **What was the consequence of Cain's sin?** (Cain was sent away to be a wanderer. The ground would no longer yield its fruit easily for Cain, just as for his father, Adam.)

Read verses 13–16.

Ask Does Cain seem sorry for his sin? Use the Faith Word Card *repentance*, and relate it to Cain's attitude. (No, he seems more worried for his life and that he will be an outcast.) **What did God do for Cain, and what does this tell us about God?** (He marked Cain to protect him. God is loving, but He doesn't like sin. He requires payment for sin.) Show the Faith Word Card *preserves*, and discuss how God preserved Cain. Point out that God preserves both the godly and ungodly. If Cain had repented, he would not have been sent away from God's presence. Instead, Cain lacked the faith to do so, and he suffered the consequences.

Finally, read Genesis 4:25. Eve understood that since Abel died and Cain was sent away, God gave Seth to fulfill His promise of a Savior. Many, many generations later, Jesus would be born as a descendant of Seth.

Review the concept of a family tree. Ask students to think of their parents, grandparents, and perhaps great-grandparents. Remind them that in God's family, we are all descendants of Adam and Eve. Direct students to the Family Tree in the Bible Discovery Guide on page 3, which shows the generations from Adam through Jacob. This line continues from Jacob to Jesus.

Teacher Tip
Look through the Divine Service liturgy for the symbol ✠ in the Invocation, the Words of Institution, and the Benediction. These indicate when it is appropriate to make the sign of the cross in remembrance of one's Baptism.

3 We Live (20 minutes)

Say God preserved Cain by marking him when He sent him away so that no one would kill him. How does God preserve us? (He cares for us and provides all things for us, including salvation through Jesus Christ.) Remind the students of the First and Second Articles, and review texts as necessary. **What mark does God place on us?** (We are marked with the sign of the cross at our Baptism. In worship, we are free to make the sign of the cross in remembrance of our Baptism.) **Both marks are marks of God's mercy, but only Baptism gives us God's complete grace for salvation. Cain's mark preserved him for this life. Baptism is God's grace for this life and for eternity.**

Ask Because he would not rely on God's grace, Cain had to pay for his own sin. Does God expect payment for our own sins? Are we able to pay for our own sins? (Yes, God expects payment. No, we could never pay for our own sins.) **Since God expects payment for sin, who pays for our sin?** (Jesus died on the cross and is the final, perfect sacrifice for our sins.) **How does this payment apply to my sin specifically?** (Through Baptism, we have received faith in Jesus Christ. We have been washed clean.) **Did God want Cain to repent and turn to Him? Does God want all people to repent and have faith?** (Yes)

Turn to page 4 of the Lesson Leaflet to read the Bible Words. Listen to and then sing the Bible Words song found on the CD, track 15. Make copies of Bible Words Puzzle 4 for students to complete now or at home.

Discuss the Faith Word Card *perish*, and review *preserves* and *repentance*.

Say For Jesus' sake, God forgives the sins of all those who repent of their sins and believe in Jesus Christ as the Savior from sin, death, and the devil. The Law shows us our sin, and we are called to repentance, realizing that we are not able to save ourselves. Faith comes from God through His Word and Holy Baptism and causes us to trust in Jesus for salvation.

Read aloud the Third Article and Explanation from Luther's Small Catechism, or use Resource Page 2 in the back of the Teacher Guide. Ask students to raise their hands or stand up when they hear the statements that stress the forgiveness of sins.

Like Cain, Like Me

Have the students turn to page 2 of the Lesson Leaflet and complete this activity as a group, discussing answers and giving further explanation. All answers are *B* with the exception of the last two, which should be *M*. Ask some students to read Matthew 5:21–22 and 1 John 3:15, and discuss. When you get to "Sent away from God's presence," explain that we are separated from God by our sins. Cain was sent away from God's presence because he was unrepentant, unfaithful, and angry at God. His reliance on himself separated him from God. Even though Cain sinned, God still loved and preserved him. Though we sin, God in Christ still loves and preserves us. He calls us to repent and gives us faith. Because of Jesus, we are forgiven of all of our sins. Jesus keeps bringing us back because He redeemed us by His death on the cross.

The answers to the two questions are *faith* and *God is patient and wants everyone to come to faith and not to perish*.

Don't Stay Angry

Say When we keep anger and hatred in our hearts, we are also guilty of breaking the Fifth Commandment. Ask a student to read the paragraph on page 3. Help the students draw the conclusion that we are just like Cain and have committed the same sins.

Conclude We are different from Cain when we repent of our sins and turn to God for forgiveness. In Baptism, God has given us faith in His Son for forgiveness, new life, and salvation. A few minutes can also be used for completing the "Don't Stay Angry!" activity.

Bible Study Skills: Bible Bingo

For Bible Study Skills Review, each student will need a Bible, a pencil, and a copy of Reproducible Page 4, found at the end of this lesson. Read the directions, and help the students create bingo cards. Encourage the students to mark their grids randomly, as this will create the necessary variable in the game. Number slips of paper 1–25, and put them into a container. Draw one slip at a time, and read the Bible reference from the reproducible page that corresponds to the number. Allow several minutes for play. Instead of awarding a prize to a single winner, consider giving participants a special bookmark for use in their

Lesson 4

Key Point
Even though Cain sinned, God still loved and preserved him. Even though we sin, God, in Christ, still loves and preserves us.

Bible, perhaps to mark a special verse or to use in their personal Bible study. Invite parents to help with the Bible Bingo activity to acknowledge the children who have located verses. This can help the game flow smoothly.

These additional suggestions may add excitement or aid students in the playing of the game. For a class that is proficient in looking up Bible verses, give a time limit for each verse—for example, twenty or thirty seconds. Have students play Bible Bingo as partners, pairing students who struggle with more proficient students. Assist students in finding the references by referring to the construction-paper bookmarks in their Bibles. For example, say "John is a Gospel" or "Psalms is a book of poetry."

4 Closing (7 minutes)

Allow five minutes or so to play one of the Bible Review Games (Resource Pages 6–8 in the back of this guide) using the Bible Review Cards introduced so far in the quarter (Bible Review Cards 1–32).

Say We, too, have sinned against the First Commandment because we have not loved God with our whole heart, mind, and soul. We, too, have sinned against the Fifth Commandment because we have killed in our thoughts and words and in actions that show our anger toward members of our families or friends. God knows our sin and sent Jesus to pay sin's penalty for us. Through Jesus, we are forgiven.

Sing again the hymn "From All That Dwell Below the Skies" (*LSB* 816; CD 1). Then, close with this prayer.

Pray Dear heavenly Father, we thank and praise You that You continually provide for our needs and preserve us in our daily lives. Thank You especially for Your Son, Jesus Christ, who was punished for our sins by His death on the cross and who rose again so that we can live eternally in heaven. Help us to be more loving to our family and friends. In Jesus' name we pray. Amen.

Bible Bingo

Write the numbers from 1 to 25 in random order in the grid below, one number on each square. Use each number only once. This will be your Bible Bingo card. Your card will be different from everyone else's card.

Your teacher will draw a number that will match one of the verses below. As quickly as you can, look up the verse in your Bible. Raise your hand and show your teacher. Then, cross the number off on your Bible Bingo card. The first one to mark off five boxes in a row—top-to-bottom, side-to-side, or corner-to-corner—is the winner.

1. Psalm 103:3–4
2. John 3:16
3. Ephesians 1:7
4. Isaiah 42:8
5. 1 Corinthians 15:22
6. Romans 10:17
7. Genesis 9:6
8. Malachi 2:10
9. Revelation 2:7
10. 1 John 2:2
11. Matthew 22:37
12. Romans 3:22–24
13. Joshua 24:14

14. 2 Corinthians 5:21
15. 1 Samuel 17:49
16. Proverbs 13:1
17. Daniel 3:26
18. Acts 4:12
19. Jonah 1:17
20. Deuteronomy 32:39
21. Luke 2:11
22. 1 John 1:8
23. Genesis 2:15
24. Colossians 1:16
25. Exodus 20:3

Reproducible Page 4 Growing in Christ® Upper Elementary © 2006, 2016 Concordia Publishing House. Reproduced by permission. This page is available on the Teacher CD.

UPPER ELEMENTARY

Preparing the Lesson

Noah and the Flood
Genesis 6:1–9:17

Lesson 5

_____
Date of Use

Key Point

In the flood, God destroyed sinful people. God's Son, Jesus, destroyed sin, once and for all, through His death and resurrection to give life to sinful people.

Law/**Gospel**

God used water in a flood to drown sinful mankind. **In Baptism, God uses water to drown my sins, granting me eternal life through His Son, Jesus.**

Context

As the tree is in the seed, so salvation history is in Genesis 1–11, including a universal judgment, a promise that a remnant shall be saved, and a new beginning.

Commentary

In Genesis 6:1–4, the "sons of God" are probably the tribe of Adam who intermarry with "daughters of man" from the tribe of Cain. When people of faith marry unbelievers, their children get the impression that faith is something optional. Genesis 6:1–6 suggests that what is important among the generations before the flood are physical attraction, "renown," deeds of strength, and the glory of the flesh.

Noah, the last of Adam's line, "found favor" and "walked with God" (6:8–9). These expressions indicate that Noah's relationship with God is one of faith. By faith, he builds the ark that God uses to save him. Noah's family apparently share his faith in God and share in the work of building and filling the ark. They are saved as part of a faith community. Noah is not a sinless man, as shown in Genesis 9:18–29.

The word *ark* is best understood as box or container. The same word is used for Moses' basket. There are two of most animals aboard the ark, but seven pairs of clean (fit to eat) animals. God plans ahead for the time after the flood.

The text shows the flood beginning and then the animals with Noah's family entering the ark. God shuts them in (7:16). The forty days of floodwaters are echoed in forty years of Israel's wandering in the wilderness, forty days of fasting by our Lord, and our forty-day Lenten season.

Floodwaters come from above as rain and from below as springs. The destruction comes not gradually but in a violent rush. The earth, including hills and mountains, is covered with water. All breathing things on "dry land" (7:22) die because of man's sin.

Genesis 8:1 is a good example of how the Bible often speaks of God in human terms: "God remembered Noah." It may have appeared that God had forgotten about Noah until God acted on the ark's behalf. Note that the ark settles in the mountains of Ararat, a region around present-day Armenia.

The raven Noah sends out fails to return because it can live off of rotting flesh; the dove returns when it finds no suitable resting place. The second time, the dove returns with an olive leaf, a sign that God is at peace with the earth and that plants useful to humans are growing once again. The third time, the dove does not need to return.

Genesis 8:17 repeats the command to be fruitful and multiply. Noah offers a sacrifice of clean animals, which God finds pleasing because of Noah's faith (Hebrews 11:7), and God resolves not to punish the earth in this way for man's sake again, observing that "man's heart is evil from his youth" (Genesis 8:21).

Some traditions believe that the rainbow existed before the flood and was given new meaning; others regard it as being created at this time. What is clear is that the rainbow is now a sign of God's peace to the world and a promise that He will not again send a worldwide flood. It is a covenant to which God binds Himself and is not dependent on human works.

The elements present in the flood—water, renewal, death because of sin, salvation because of being joined to the people of faith, and God's unconditional promise of grace—are present in the Sacrament of Baptism (1 Peter 3:18–21).

To hear an in-depth discussion of this Bible account, visit cph.org/podcast and listen to our Seeds of Faith podcast each week.

Lesson 5
Noah and the Flood
Genesis 6:1–9:17

Connections

Bible Words
The Lord will rescue me from every evil deed and bring me safely into His heavenly kingdom. To Him be the glory forever and ever. Amen. 2 Timothy 4:18

Faith Words
Baptism, redemption, salvation, covenant

Hymn
God's Own Child, I Gladly Say It (*LSB* 594:1, 5; CD 2)

Catechism
Holy Baptism

Liturgy
Baptismal font

1 Opening (7 minutes)

Before this lesson, check with parents, the Sunday School superintendent, or the church secretary to find out the dates of your students' Baptisms. Some children may remember the date of their Baptism; others may not. Near the end of the "We Live" section, students will have opportunity to write this date in their leaflet.

Welcome your students, introducing any new students. Take attendance, and collect the offering. Make copies of Bible Words Puzzle 5 for students to complete as they wait for class to begin.

If possible, take your students into the sanctuary for the opening and to look at the baptismal font. Take with you this Teacher Guide; Faith Word Cards (*Baptism, redemption, salvation*); and any necessary materials for singing the hymn. Continue when all students are quietly seated in church.

Baptism Memories

Say **Do any of you remember your Baptism?** Allow for responses. If possible, show a picture from your own Baptism and relate any memories you have from that day. For example, my mom always told me how hot it was that day; when my son was baptized, he wore the Baptism outfit that his dad wore; and the like.

Ask **What happens during a Baptism?** Responses might include something about the pastor putting water on a baby. **Why does the pastor put water on the baby?** Show Faith Word Card *Baptism*, and have a student read the definition. **What is special about this kind of bath or washing?** Allow for responses.

MATERIALS NEEDED

1 Opening
Teacher Tools
CD
Faith Word Cards 17–19
Other Supplies
Baptismal memento (optional)

2 God Speaks
Teacher Tools
Faith Word Card 18
Poster B
Student Stuff
Lesson Leaflets
Bible Discovery Guides
Other Supplies
Reproducible Page 5 (TG)
Blue construction paper
Resource Pages 6–8 (TG; optional)

3 We Live
Teacher Tools
Faith Word Card 17, 20
Student Stuff
Lesson Leaflets
Other Supplies
Resource Page 4 (TG)
Shells or poster board (optional)

4 Closing
Teacher Tools
CD
Faith Word Cards
Other Supplies
Damp paper towels

Say Baptism is a special kind of bath. It's not a bath that washes dirt away. The water used in Baptism is regular water. But the water attached to God's promise in His Word washes away sin. Because of our sinful nature, we sin in our thoughts, in our words, and in the things we do. But Baptism washes away those sins. Because of Jesus' death on the cross and His resurrection, God saves us through the forgiving bath of Baptism. On the anniversary of your Baptism each year, you can remember the special way God has saved you from your sins in Baptism. But every day, and especially when you hear or say the Invocation and make the sign of the cross, you can remember the forgiveness you have in Jesus Christ.

Play and sing the hymn "God's Own Child, I Gladly Say It" (*LSB* 594:1, 5; CD 2), and discuss the references in the hymn to Baptism. Review stanza 1, and focus on the words *redemption* and *salvation*, using the Faith Word Cards.

Pray Dear Lord, thank You for the gift of Baptism, through which You forgive us and save us. We pray that You would help us every day to be sorry for our sins and to trust in You for forgiveness. Every day, help us remember how much You love us—You sent your only Son, Jesus, to die for our sins. Through Christ we pray. Amen.

2 God Speaks (23 minutes)

The Scripture lesson for today is a long, three-chapter section from Genesis. The lesson can be taught using the portions of the text given, or the Bible text can be read in its entirety. You decide which option is best for your students.

Noah's Story

Distribute copies of Reproducible Page 5, found at the end of this lesson, with the story sequence cards to students. Have them cut apart the cards and arrange them in the correct order.

Say Our lesson today about Noah and the flood will help us see that the flood was a type of Baptism. The flood in the Old Testament foreshadowed, or pointed to, Holy Baptism in the New Testament.

Ask What does *foreshadowed* mean? Allow for responses, and then present this analogy. **Have you ever been somewhere on a sunny day where you can see a shadow on the ground, but you can't see who or what is making the shadow because something is blocking that person or object from your view?** Elicit a few responses. **Or let's say that you're walking down a city street at night, and as you approach a corner, you see light from a streetlight that is hidden from view around the corner. Then you notice a person's shadow in that patch of light, and you know someone is standing just around the corner. You can't see the person, but you know he or she is there because you see the shadow. Was the shadow the *real* thing, or was it a *type* of the real thing pointing to the real thing?** This should prompt some discussion. (The *shadow* pointed you in the right direction. You saw the shadow *before* you saw the real thing. The silhouette on the sidewalk *foreshadowed* the actual person.) While you are answering the last question, you may want to write the italicized words on the board as you emphasize them so the students can see the connection.

Liturgy Link

Many baptismal fonts have eight sides, symbolic of the eight faithful survivors of the flood and the "eighth day of creation" when God began the world anew with Noah and his family. Our Baptism enables us to begin again. We are raised new creatures from the waters of the font. Before, we were dead in sin, but now, we are alive in Christ.

Key Point

In the flood, God destroyed sinful people. God's Son, Jesus, destroyed sin, once and for all, by His death and resurrection to give life to sinful people.

Lesson 5

Key Point
In the flood, God destroyed sinful people. God's Son, Jesus, destroyed sin, once and for all, by His death and resurrection to give life to sinful people.

Say Now, see if you can figure out how the flood foreshadowed Baptism as we study God's Word. Before we read Noah's story, let's see how many of you can put these story sequence cards in the correct order. Allow students time to complete the activity. Ask them to keep their cards in order until the end of the lesson.

The Flood and Noah

Say Open your Bibles to Genesis 6. Distribute Lesson Leaflets, and direct students to the top of page 2. Create similar boxes on a chalkboard or whiteboard so students can use your written responses as a guide.

Say In your Lesson Leaflet, you will fill in the boxes shown as we answer the questions. Let's look at the first box on the left, which says "What went wrong?" Think about that as we study portions of the story in Genesis. Ask a student volunteer to read Genesis 6:5–10. Let's hear again what God says in verse 5: "The Lord saw that the wickedness of man was great in the earth, and that every intention of the thoughts of his heart was only evil continually." So, what went wrong? What is the problem shown in these verses? (Men were wicked; the thoughts of man were evil.)

Ask Were the hearts of people good some of the time, but they just did a lot of bad things? Allow responses. Verse 5 is clear that the nature of men ("every intention of the thoughts of his heart") was sinful or evil all of the time. God shows in these verses that men were sinful in their nature. From this sinful nature came evil thoughts, evil words, and evil deeds. So, what could we write in our first box? Allow for responses. In your first box, write: Man was wicked.

Now, let's read Genesis 6:13, 17 to discover the result of the wickedness of man. Ask a student volunteer to read those verses. (God had to destroy sin. He decided to make a flood.) God had to destroy sin in a flood. Encourage students to fill in the second box entitled, "What is the result?" In your second box, write: God must destroy sin.

Continue reading the Bible verses and filling in the boxes in this manner.

What was God's promise to Noah? Allow for responses, and then read Genesis 6:18–7:5 either together or in small groups. (God's promise to Noah was that He would rescue Noah because of Noah's faith.) In the third box, write: God promised to rescue Noah.

What happened at the end of Noah's story? Read together or in small groups Genesis 8:1, 20–22; 9:8–17. Invite students to respond to the question. Review Genesis 8:1, if necessary. What happens to Noah after the flood? (God remembered Noah [Genesis 8:1].) God kept His promise that He would rescue Noah through the flood. What else does God promise at the end of the story? (At the end of Noah's story, God remembers His promise to Noah and rescues him from the flood. God makes a covenant with Noah [Genesis 9:13–16].) In the fourth box, write: God remembered Noah and made a covenant with him.

Using the Faith Word Card *covenant*, review this definition with your students. A *covenant* is a formal, binding agreement between two or more people or groups.

Ask What covenant did God make with Noah? Allow for responses. (God's covenant or agreement with Noah is that He would never again make the waters into a flood to destroy all flesh [Genesis 9:15].)

Growing in CHRIST.

Locate Mount Ararat on Poster B.

Say It says in Genesis 8:4 that Noah's ark "came to rest on the mountains of Ararat." There is a mountain by that name in modern-day Turkey, and many people have spent a lot of time trying to dig for remains of the ark there, but no conclusive evidence has been found to show where Noah landed. God's Word, however, is real and true, and the events of the Bible happened in real places and times. The Bible is not contradicted by world history.

Fascinating Facts

Have the students turn in their Bible Discovery Guides to pages 8–9. In pairs, have students look through the captions and photos. Then, assign these questions to different pairs:

Which picture of Noah's ark is the most accurate, according to Genesis? (The picture of the more "boxy" looking ship)

How big was Noah's ark? (450 feet long, 75 feet wide, 45 feet high)

How does the size of Noah's ark compare to a tennis court? (Noah's ark is bigger in square footage than twelve tennis courts put together.)

Which animals did Noah take on the ark? ("Take with you seven pairs of all clean animals, the male and his mate, and a pair of the animals that are not clean, the male and his mate, and seven pairs of the birds of the heavens also, male and female, to keep their offspring alive on the face of all the earth" Genesis 7:2–3.)

What about fish and whales? (Creatures that lived in the water didn't need to board the ark!)

Reviewing Noah's Story

Say **Let's see if you arranged your cards in the proper sequence. What is the correct order of the story sequence cards?** (The correct order follows. [1] Everyone sinned and did what was evil in God's eyes. [2] God told Noah to build an ark. [3] Pairs of every animal got on the ark. [4] It rained for forty days. [5] A dove found an olive branch and brought it to Noah. [6] God saved Noah.) Direct your students' attention to the cover picture on their leaflet. **What has the artist shown?** (Noah and his family are worshiping God.) Read Genesis 8:18–22.

Give students a piece of blue construction paper so they can glue the story sequence cards to it in the correct order.

The Bible Review Cards can be used to review the basic facts of the story. They may be used with one of the Bible Review Games (Resource Pages 6–8 at the back of this guide). As another option, if time allows, the cards could be used as a "search-and-find" activity. In order to do this, write the eight Bible verses on a chalkboard or whiteboard that reveal the answers to the questions. Students would then try to match the correct Bible verse with the question. The Bible references are (1) Genesis 6:5–7; (2) Genesis 6:14; (3) Genesis 7:13; (4) Genesis 6:19–21; (5) Genesis 7:17; (6) Genesis 8:11; (7) Genesis 8:19–20; and (8) Genesis 9:13. Scramble the questions when asking the students so it is not obvious which reference corresponds to which question.

Lesson 5

3 We Live (15 minutes)

Key Point
In the flood, God destroyed sinful people. God's Son, Jesus, destroyed sin, once and for all, by His death and resurrection to give life to sinful people.

Saving Waters

Ask Have you figured out how the flood foreshadowed Baptism? Review the meaning of *Baptism*. (God used water in a flood to drown sinful man. In Baptism, God uses water to drown my sins, granting me eternal life through Jesus.)

Continue with the activity at the top of page 3 in the Lesson Leaflet. Read the words of 1 Peter 3:21 in the arc over the top of the shell together. "Baptism . . . now saves you . . . through the resurrection of Jesus Christ."

Say In the flood, God destroyed sinful people but rescued Noah and his family. Jesus, His Son, destroyed sin, once and for all, by His death and resurrection to give life to sinful people, rescuing us from sin and death.

Direct the students to the Bible Words on page 4 of the leaflet. To aid in memorization, write the words of 2 Timothy 4:18 on several sheets of paper, according to the number of students in your class, including the Bible reference on one sheet, and give each sheet to a student. Challenge them to arrange themselves in the correct order to display the verse to the rest of the class. Then, have students read the verse together. Direct one student to take his or her word out of place and sit down and have students again read the verse, supplying the missing word. Prompt them as needed. Continue removing one or two words and having students read the verse, filling in the missing words. Finally, when the Bible reference and all the words of the verse are gone, see if the class can recite the entire verse. Ask for volunteers to recite the Bible verse alone.

Using the Faith Word Cards, review the words *Baptism* and *salvation* as they complete the rest of the baptismal shell. Help your students, as needed, to fill in information about their Baptism dates. (If you were not able to obtain a list of Baptism dates for your students, suggest that the students work with their parents to locate and fill in the information at home.) Invite students to color or decorate their shell on their Lesson Leaflet.

A Great Idea!
Or obtain a fan-shaped shell for each of your students; they are available at some craft stores. Let the students use permanent markers to write their names and Baptism dates on the inside surface of a shell. (Or cut similar shapes from poster board for the students to personalize and decorate.)

Say At the beginning of our lesson today, we talked about the benefits of Baptism. Who can tell me something that Baptism does? Allow for responses.

Make a copy of Resource Page 4 for each student, found in the back of the Teacher Guide. Read together the Second Part of Baptism. Have students work together on the fill-in-the-blank activity at the bottom of page 2 in the Lesson Leaflet. Correct answers are *forgiveness, rescues, death, devil, eternal, salvation,* and *promises*.

4 Closing (5 minutes)

Play the catechism songs from tracks 19 and 20 of the CD. Ask how these sections of the First Article might relate to what the students have learned about Noah and Baptism. Sing these two parts of the First Article.

Practice reciting the books of the Bible together to continue to aid in memorization. Review Faith Words by challenging students to spell some of the words used in Lessons 1–5. Select words for students according to level of difficulty, or start with shorter words and work up to longer, more difficult words.

Give each student a wipe or damp paper towel. Ask students to wipe down their table area or desk, making it clean. Connect how God made the world clean again and how He makes us clean too.

Sing again the hymn "God's Own Child, I Gladly Say It" (*LSB* 594:1, 5; CD 2).

Pray Dear Lord Jesus, thank You for Your Word, which teaches about how You rescued Noah from the flood. Thank You for rescuing me and washing my sins away in Baptism. Please help me to remember my Baptism and to be thankful because of Your great love. In Jesus' name I pray. Amen.

Say This week, remember that God has forgiven and saved you and loves you very much!

Noah's Story
Story Sequence Cards

God told Noah to build an ark.

A dove found an olive branch and brought it to Noah.

God saved Noah and his family.

Everyone sinned and did what was evil in God's eyes.

Pairs of every animal got on the ark.

It rained for forty days.

UPPER ELEMENTARY

Preparing the Lesson

God's Covenant with Abram

Genesis 12:1–9; 15:1–6; 17

Lesson 6

Date of Use

Key Point

God chose Abram (Abraham) and gave him faith to trust His promises to save His people. God gives us faith in Jesus, our Savior.

Law/Gospel

In my sin, I doubt that God can do what He promises and do not trust Him. **God in His mercy carries out His promises and gives me faith in and through Jesus to trust Him.**

Context

Genesis 1–11 describes the creation of the world and the history of all humanity. Genesis 12 begins a new era. God calls one person, Abram, to be the physical and spiritual father of His chosen people. God will work through Abram and his descendants to bring salvation for all. Abram's line culminates in Jesus Christ (Matthew 1:1–2; Romans 9:5), the offspring promised to Eve. True God and true man, Jesus brings forgiveness of sins and eternal life to all believers. All who are baptized into Christ are Abram's spiritual offspring and heirs of God's promises to Abram (Galatians 3:26–29).

Commentary

In Genesis 12, God calls Abram to leave his homeland and go to a new land. Abram must travel and live by faith, since he does not know where God will lead him. God promises to bless others through Abram and his offspring.

In Genesis 15, the word of the Lord comes to Abram in a vision, assuring him there is nothing to fear. But Abram does fear because he has no son. God tells Abram to number the stars and promises that his offspring will be as numerous as those stars. "And [Abram] believed the Lord, and He counted it to him as righteousness" (Genesis 15:6). Paul quotes this verse in Romans 4:3 and Galatians 3:6 to show that Abram was justified—that is, declared righteous before God—not by works, but by faith in God's promises, including the promise of the Savior, who was to come from Abram's own descendants.

The Lord assures Abram that He will give him the land of Canaan. Abram asks how he can be certain. God pledges His faithfulness by means of a covenant in which God confirms His promises with a solemn ceremony that includes sacrifice. The Lord tells Abram that after his descendants have sojourned in another land for four hundred years, God will give them Canaan as their possession.

As time elapses, Sarai remains childless, so she gives her maidservant Hagar to Abram so that Hagar might bear him a son. Ishmael is born when Abram is eighty-six. When Abram is ninety-nine years old, God changes his name from Abram ("exalted father") to Abraham ("father of a multitude"). God seals His covenant with Abraham by telling him that he and all of his male descendants are to be circumcised as "a sign of the covenant between Me and you" (17:11).

God also changes Sarai's name to Sarah (both mean "princess") and promises that kings shall come from her. Abraham laughs, perhaps in joyful confidence that the Lord will perform this miracle or perhaps with a degree of skepticism. Abraham then asks for God's blessing on Ishmael.

God confirms that He will indeed bless Ishmael but that He will establish His everlasting covenant with a son born to Sarah (to be named Isaac). Through Isaac, God would fulfill His greatest promise: that from Abraham and Sarah's descendants would be born the Savior, Jesus, in whom all the nations of the earth would be blessed through the forgiveness of sins.

To hear an in-depth discussion of this Bible account, visit cph.org/podcast and listen to our Seeds of Faith podcast each week.

Lesson 6

God's Covenant with Abram

Genesis 12:1–9; 15:1–6; 17

Connections

Bible Words
No one can say "Jesus is Lord" except in the Holy Spirit. 1 Corinthians 12:3 (CD 12)

Faith Words
promise, descendant, fulfillment, doctrine

Hymn
How Firm a Foundation (*LSB* 728; CD 3)

Catechism
Apostles' Creed: Third Article

Teacher Tip

If you have a student with disabilities, be sure to keep lines of communication open with the parents. Ask them what is reasonable to expect from their child in terms of which activities the child is able to participate in and which rules the child should be expected to follow.

1 Opening (5 minutes)

Use the Faith Word Cards for this lesson in a matching activity prior to the beginning of the lesson. Before students arrive, attach (so that they can be easily removed) the four cards to the left side of the chalkboard or whiteboard with the definition side showing. On the right side of the board, write the four Faith Words in a scrambled order. Have students draw a line from the definition to the word they think it matches. As the lesson progresses, cards can be removed to see if they were matched correctly.

Welcome students to your classroom. If you haven't already, make sure you establish a predictable routine for your students as you begin your lesson.

Say In the name of the Father and of the Son and of the Holy Spirit. Amen.

Before you sing the hymn "How Firm a Foundation," look at the lyrics.

Discuss Which stanzas of this hymn make you think of the word *promise* (one of our Faith Words today)? (Stanzas 2, 3, 4, and 5 all rehearse God's promises to us.) Remove the Faith Word Card showing the definition that is matched to *promise*, and read the definition aloud. **Today, we'll talk about God's promises to Abram (A bruhm). In this hymn, what is promised to all God's people?** (God will support us in all trials and take us to heaven because of His grace.)

Play and sing the hymn, CD track 3.

Pray Dear Father in heaven, thank You for caring for Your people and for blessing us with faith. Please help us grow in our faith today as we study Your words for us. Through Christ we pray. Amen.

MATERIALS NEEDED

1 Opening	2 God Speaks	3 We Live	4 Closing
Teacher Tools	**Teacher Tools**	**Teacher Tools**	**Teacher Tools**
Faith Word Cards 21–24	Faith Word Cards 18, 22	Faith Word Cards 23, 24	Bible Review Cards 1–48
CD	Posters A and B	Poster C	CD
	Student Stuff	CD	**Other Supplies**
	Lesson Leaflets	**Student Stuff**	Construction paper (optional)
		Lesson Leaflets	
		Bible Discovery Guides	

2 God Speaks (20 minutes)

Begin your lesson today with a discussion about names and nicknames. Distribute small pieces of paper and pencils.

Say **If you could choose any name for yourself, what would it be?** Suggest funny nicknames such as Captain Collision, Super Slugger, Neat Nellie, and the like. Allow students to write their response on the paper.

Ask **Why did you choose your name?** Students might respond by saying that their names tell something about themselves. For example, Captain Collision is always falling and getting hurt. Super Slugger is a power hitter on the baseball team and so forth.

Say **Today, we're going to learn about God's covenant promises for Abram. We'll also learn about how God changes Abram's name.** Review the Faith Word *covenant* introduced in Lesson 5.

On the timeline poster, Poster A, point to the dates shown for Abram, Ishmael (IHSH may ell), and Isaac as these encompass the chapters covered in today's lesson. (Although the birth of Ishmael is not a key part of this lesson, it may be of interest to your students. Ishmael's birth is noted in Genesis 16.) Abram is about eighty-five years old now. Point out on Poster B that God called Abram while he was in Haran (HAIR uhn); then he traveled south into Canaan (KANE un) and lived in many places.

God's Promises to Abram

Have students open their Bibles to Genesis 15 and page 2 of the Lesson Leaflet. Have students volunteer to read the passages in Part A and to find God's promise to Abram in each.

Part A

1. Genesis 15:1   (e) I am your shield; your reward shall be very great.

2. Genesis 15:2–4   (a) Your very own son shall be your heir.

Before reading Genesis 15:5, distribute copies of Reproducible Page 6, found at the end of this lesson. It is an activity that is a paraphrase of verse 5.

3. Genesis 15:5   (f) Your offspring shall be as numerous as the stars in the sky. (See picture on page 1 of the Lesson Leaflet.)

After completing Part A, check the Faith Word Card *descendant* on the board. Read the definition together.

Say **At this time in his life, did Abram have descendants?** (Sarai [SARE eye] was barren, unable to have children, before God's promise to her.) **What was God's promise to Abram regarding descendants?** (God said that Abram would have as many descendants as the stars.) **Why did this promise confuse Abram?** (Abram and Sarai had no children, and they were old. He wondered how they could still have descendants when his wife was past the age of childbearing.) **Did God's promises always make sense to Abram?** (No)

Say **Even when God makes promises that seem impossible, remember: He is God, and He can do things that to us seem like they could never happen.**

Ask **How would you describe God's relationship with Abram based upon what you know about God and His promises?** (God could be trusted; God

---

Lesson 6

Key Point
God gave Abram (Abraham) faith to trust His promises to save His people. God gives us faith in Jesus, our Savior.

Teacher Tip
Make things just a little simpler for students who have learning disabilities by having a volunteer read the Bible portions aloud. Don't necessarily expect everyone to read a portion.

Lesson 6

Key Point
God gave Abram (Abraham) faith to trust His promises to save His people. God gives us faith in Jesus, our Savior.

provided for Abram; He is full of grace; He gave Abram many blessings. God is always faithful to His promises.) **Let's read another verse in Genesis 15.** Read Genesis 15:6 together. **How did Abram become righteous? Was it because of something he did?** (No. He was righteous because of faith.) **This verse says that because Abram believed the Lord and His promises, he was considered righteous by God.**

Say **Abram could have doubted God. In fact, he asked God how he would know for sure that he would possess the land God had promised to him. It seemed like the things God was promising could never happen. Abram and his wife were old. His wife was past the age of childbearing. But Abram believed that God could do what He had promised. Turn in your Bibles to Romans 4:18–24.** Read the passage together. **Look again at verse 21. What does it say about what Abram believed in?** (It says that Abram was "fully convinced that God was able to do what He had promised.") **Abram's faith was based in God's promises. God promised to be gracious and to bless Abram, and Abram—by God's grace—placed His faith in these promises from God. God's promises were the beginning of Abram's faith. God gave faith to Abram and not only made promises, but also kept those promises.**

Explain **Genesis 16 tells us that Sarai and Abram tried to help God instead of waiting on God's timing to fulfill His promises. They doubted God's promises. But God forgave their sin of doubting and kept His covenant promise to save His people through Abram's descendant.**

Have students silently read along as you read aloud Genesis 17:1–8.

Say **Abraham's new name is tied to God's promise to make Abraham a great nation. Within this promise of descendants is also another promise. God was promising that one of Abraham's descendants would be very special. Who is God referring to?** Allow students to consider the question. **Yes, a descendant of Abraham, almost two thousand years later, would be Jesus, God's only Son. The Bible traces Jesus' family line way back to Abraham, and even further back to Noah and to Adam and Eve.**

See "God's Family Tree" as you look at the genealogy of Jesus in Matthew 1:1–2, 16–17. You may want to write "Abram/Abraham" and "Sarai/Sarah" on the board.

Say **Often, Hebrew names have special meanings and tell something about the person. The name *Abram* meant "exalted father." Then God changed his name to *Abraham*, "father of a multitude." Both *Sarai* and *Sarah* meant "princess." God promised Abraham and Sarah that kings and the King of kings, Jesus, would come from their family. This promise was so special that God gave Abraham and Sarah new names to mark the occasion.**

Continue with Part B in the Lesson Leaflet.

4. Genesis 17:15–16 (b) God will bless Sarai; God would give Abram a son through her; from her will come kings of people.

5. Genesis 17:17–19 (g) Your wife Sarah will bear a son, that you should call Isaac.

6. Genesis 17:20 (d) God will bless Ishmael; he will be the father of twelve princes.

7. Genesis 17:21 (c) God will establish His covenant with Abraham's son Isaac.

Growing in CHRIST

Lesson 6

3 We Live (15 minutes)

God's Promises to Me

If possible, take your students into the sanctuary for this brief portion of the lesson. Gather them around the baptismal font.

 A Great Idea!

Say **In Genesis 15:7–21, God restated His promise of giving the land to Abraham and gave him a visible symbol that He knew Abraham would understand, because it was the way people made covenants in the land of Ur where Abraham had come from. It was God's way of guaranteeing to Abraham that His promises were sure and real.** Read these verses to the children without dwelling on them. Be prepared for students' queries in regard to this section. **God's promises to Abraham, sealed in a covenant, are similar to Baptism and the Lord's Supper.** Challenge the students to make the comparison. (In these Sacraments, God speaks the message of His mercy in Christ [forgiveness and life in the promised land of heaven] and He gives us something to see—water, bread, and wine—to make it all the more sure for us. In this visible sign, God binds Himself to His promise. That is evidence of His grace.) **Have you heard the pastor announce the name of a child or adult when they are baptized?** Accept responses. **"Giving" someone their name at Baptism is a custom that reminds us that in Baptism we are made new. Our sins are washed away. We are made children of God. We are given faith to trust in Christ. That's a wonderful blessing. In one sense, each of us was renamed "Christian" at our Baptism.**

God's Plan

Direct the students to the illustration on page 3 of the leaflet. Remind them that God promised that Abram would become a great nation. In Genesis 15, God tells Abram that the number of his descendants would be like that of stars in the sky.

Ask **Who was Abram's most important descendant?** (Jesus, the Christ) **Christ was the descendant who was born to break sin's hold over each of us. Christ was the fulfillment of God's plan of salvation for mankind.**

Review with the students the meaning of the Faith Word *fulfillment*.

Within the stars are words and numbers. Have the students write the words on the numbered blanks below the picture. When completed, the message should read *He remembers His covenant forever, the word that He commanded, for a thousand generations, the covenant that He made with Abraham* (Psalm 105:8–9a).

Point out to your students that God still keeps the covenant He made with Abram (who later is renamed Abraham).

Say **By faith, given to us in Baptism and nurtured in us by God's Word and the Lord's Supper, we are spiritual descendants of Abram and ones who receive the blessings God promised, especially the blessings of forgiveness, new life, and salvation in Jesus Christ.**

Like Abram, we sin when we fail to trust God's leading of our lives, questioning His directions and failing to follow Him.

www.cph.org

Lesson 6

Ask What are some ways that young people your age are like Abram, sinful and distrustful of God? Allow time for volunteers to respond. If needed, offer these examples: **We rebel against our parents and fail to honor our teachers. We give in to peer pressure instead of making God-pleasing decisions in life. Yet God still promises to guide and bless us and does so through His Son. Like Abram, we are sinful people and deserve eternal death and damnation as the penalty for our sins. But Abram's most important descendant, Jesus, is, by God's gift of faith, our Savior from sin. Though we sin daily and even our best efforts to please God are spoiled by poor motives and failures, Jesus stands by our side before God and makes us pleasing to Him.**

Say **Let's read with our eyes as we listen with our ears to our Bible Words.** "No one can say 'Jesus is Lord' except in the Holy Spirit" (1 Corinthians 12:3). Play the Bible Words song on track 12. Make copies of Bible Words Puzzle 6 for students to complete now or at home.

Ask **Who can tell me in your own words what this Bible verse means?** (No one can be a Christian without the Holy Spirit converting us.)

Refer to Faith Word Card *doctrine*.

Key Point
God gave Abram (Abraham) faith to trust His promises to save His people. God gives us faith in Jesus, our Savior.

Say **The Bible is our only source for the clear teachings of the Church, what we call "doctrines" from the Latin word for *teaching*. We have those doctrines explained for us in Luther's Small Catechism. It has six chief (important) parts. Who can name them?** Give several children opportunities to name all of the parts. Use Poster C as a helpful tool. Direct students to page 4 of their Lesson Leaflets.

Say **When we say the Apostles' Creed, which is a summary of the doctrines taught by the apostles Jesus chose, we are acknowledging that we cannot believe in Jesus on our own.** The Third Article is printed in the Lesson Leaflet on page 3; direct the students to find it and to follow along as you continue.

In the explanation, we say, "I believe that I cannot by my own reason or strength believe in Jesus Christ, my Lord, or come to Him; but the Holy Spirit has called me by the Gospel, enlightened me with His gifts, sanctified and kept me in the true faith." What is reason? (Being able to think clearly through arguments, understanding things) **What is strength?** (My abilities, either physical or some other way) **This portion of Luther's explanation of the Third Article says I cannot believe in Jesus on my own. I can't decide that I want to believe in Jesus. The Holy Spirit does the work. I don't have the capability to trust in Christ on my own. Instead, God gives the promises of salvation and eternal life and then provides me with the faith to believe His promises.**

Temporary/Permanent Dwellings

Pages 12–13 in the Bible Discovery Guide give information about the nomadic life of Abraham and other people of Old Testament times. Direct the students to work with a partner to read the information about dwelling in tents. After reading both pages,

Explain Our lives are, in some ways, like Abraham's. He lived in a tent and moved around. He had no permanent home. We are not in our permanent home yet either. Let's suppose you went on a trip to another country. Once there, you couldn't speak the language of the people, and the food and the way the people did things were different from what you were familiar with. **How would you feel?** Allow for brief discussion. **You would probably feel strange and uncomfortable because you weren't in your own home. But when you go to heaven, you will be in your permanent home, where Jesus has prepared a place for you. How do you think you will feel in your permanent home in heaven?** Allow for more brief discussion. **Before Jesus began His suffering for the punishment of our sins, He gave His disciples and us these words of comfort from John 14:2–3.** Ask someone to read the text.

Ask **What does Jesus mean?** (He would rise again from the dead and ascend to heaven. He promised to return to earth to take us to heaven.) **We remember that God always keeps His promises and that He gives us the faith to believe in Him. We will be with Him in heaven someday.**

4 Closing (10 minutes)

Use the Bible Review Cards for this lesson and any previous lessons to review some of the factual information from the Bible story. Use any game format described in previous lessons, as time allows. Sing "How Firm a Foundation" (*LSB* 728; CD 3) and Luther's Morning Prayer (CD 21).

Pass out construction paper and markers. Remind the class that you are all part of Abraham's family as believers in Christ, the Promised One. In fact, your congregation is a big family of brothers and sisters in Christ. Ask students to create a card for a brother or sister in Christ. A possible message would be "Thank you for being in my church family!" or "I am your (brother/sister) in Christ!" If students are going to worship after this class, encourage them to give their card to someone they see there.

Pray Dear Father, thank You for teaching us in Your Word about Abraham and the faith You gave him. Thank You for giving us the gift of faith through Baptism and through the hearing of Your Word. Thank You for forgiving us when we doubt Your promises. Please increase our faith and help us tell others about the good news of salvation found only in Jesus. In His name we pray. Amen.

God's Promise to Abraham
Genesis 15:5

Abram and Sarai's tent was empty. No little boys shouted with joy. No little girls giggled with happiness.

One day, God made a promise to Abram. God told him how many descendants (children and grandchildren and great-grandchildren and great-great-grandchildren) he would have. And even though his tent was still empty, Abram believed God would keep His promise.

In each star, circle the word that doesn't belong. Then, begin in the top left star and read the circled words to find out how many descendants (offspring) God told Abram to expect.

Reproducible Page 6 Growing in Christ® Upper Elementary © 2006, 2016 Concordia Publishing House. Scripture: ESV®. Reproduced by permission. This page is available on the Teacher CD.

UPPER ELEMENTARY

Preparing the Lesson
Abraham's Visitors from Heaven
Genesis 18:1–15; 21:1–7

Lesson 7

_____
Date of Use

Key Point
God came to Abraham with the promise of a son. Abraham's descendant, our Lord Jesus, comes to us in Word and Sacraments, telling us that in Him all things are possible.

Law/**Gospel**
I sin by doubting God's Word and promises, thinking He cannot do what He says. **As God's child, I have nothing to fear because God is faithful and His Word is true. He has kept His promise to send His Son, Jesus, to be my Savior, and through Him, He gives me the joy of His salvation.**

Context
In Genesis 17, God had promised Abraham: "Sarah your wife shall bear you a son, and you shall call his name Isaac. . . . I will establish My covenant with Isaac, whom Sarah shall bear to you at this time next year" (vv. 19, 21). Now, the Lord reaffirms that promise.

Commentary
While Abraham is sitting by the door of his tent in the heat of the day, three visitors appear. One of them is identified in Genesis 18:1, 10, 13, and 14 as "the Lord" (Yahweh). The other two are angels (Genesis 19:1). Abraham shows his guests legendary Middle Eastern hospitality by arranging for a meal for them. The writer to the Hebrews encourages us to do likewise: "Do not neglect to show hospitality to strangers, for thereby some have entertained angels unawares" (13:2).

Abraham arranges a generous feast and stands humbly by, taking the role of a servant while his guests eat. The guests then ask the whereabouts of Sarah, who is listening from the tent. Sarah hears the Lord repeat His promise that He will return to Abraham about this time next year and that Sarah will give birth to a son. Since Sarah is well past her childbearing years, she laughs in disbelief.

The omniscient Lord, however, knows about her laughter and the underlying unbelief, and He addresses her through Abraham: "Why did Sarah laugh and say, 'Shall I indeed bear a child, now that I am old?'" (Genesis 18:13). The gracious Lord is not interested in exposing Sarah's unbelief for the sake of shaming her, but in order that she might recognize her sinful unbelief and turn from it to faith in God's promises and His power to accomplish them. He continues, "Is anything too hard for the Lord? At the appointed time I will return to you, about this time next year, and Sarah shall have a son" (18:14).

However, Sarah still tries to cover up her sin and denies laughing. The Lord again confronts her with His knowledge that she did laugh. The name God decreed for her son (17:19), Isaac, means "he laughs." It will be a lifelong reminder to her both of her sinful mistrust and of the Lord's mercy to her in spite of it. The writer to the Hebrews tells us that the Lord did kindle faith in Sarah: "By faith Sarah herself received power to conceive, even when she was past the age, since she considered Him faithful who had promised" (11:11).

Genesis 21 records the fulfillment of God's promise. The Lord visited Sarah in grace and enabled her to give birth to Isaac, the son through whom God would ultimately fulfill His greatest promise to Abraham. God would bless all the families of the earth (Genesis 12:3) with salvation by sending Jesus, "the son of Isaac, the son of Abraham" (Luke 3:34), "the son of God" (3:38).

To hear an in-depth discussion of this Bible account, visit cph.org/podcast and listen to our Seeds of Faith podcast each week.

Lesson 7
Abraham's Visitors from Heaven
Genesis 18:1–15; 21:1–7

Connections

Bible Words
With God all things are possible. Matthew 19:26

Faith Words
omniscient, unbelief, sanctification, saint

Hymn
If God Himself Be for Me (*LSB* 724; CD 4)

Catechism
Lord's Prayer: Second Petition

1 Opening (5 minutes)

Welcome students to your classroom. Make copies of Bible Words Puzzle 7 for students to complete as they wait to begin the lesson.

Begin with the Invocation. Then lead the students in opening prayer.

Say In the name of the Father and of the Son and of the Holy Spirit. Amen.

Pray Dear Lord, thank You for Your constant blessings. Thank You for being with us and for reassuring us of Your care. Help us learn today about how You fulfilled Your Word to Abraham and Sarah. Help us to trust You and to hear Your words of grace and forgiveness so that we never have to be afraid because of our sinfulness. In Jesus' name we pray. Amen.

Have a "Joke Contest." Invite each student to stand in front of the class and share a riddle or "Knock, Knock" joke. Emphasize, if necessary, that it should be appropriate to share in Sunday School.

Ask What are times that you might laugh? (When you hear a joke, when something funny happens) **Can you think of ways in which our laughing might be sinful? In other words, are there some things we shouldn't laugh at?** (We shouldn't laugh at people when they get hurt, we shouldn't laugh to make fun of people, etc.) **Have you ever laughed when someone tells you something that you don't think is true?** (Accept responses.)

Today, we're going to hear about some laughter in the Bible. We'll also learn that although God hates sin, He is "gracious and merciful, slow to anger and abounding in steadfast love" (Psalm 145:8). He punished His own Son for our sins, destroying sin by Jesus' suffering and death on the cross.

MATERIALS NEEDED

1 Opening
Teacher Tools
CD

2 God Speaks
Teacher Tools
Faith Word Cards 25–28
Bible Review Cards 49–56
Posters A and B

Student Stuff
Lesson Leaflets
Bible Discovery Guide

Other Supplies
Fresh cheese curds or cottage cheese (optional)

3 We Live
Teacher Tools
Faith Word Cards 27–28

Student Stuff
Lesson Leaflets

Other Supplies
Reproducible Page 7 (TG)

4 Closing
Teacher Tools
CD

Student Stuff
Lesson Leaflets

Lesson 7

② **God Speaks** (20 minutes)

God's Grace and Mercy

Display the Faith Word Cards for this lesson in this order (*omniscient, unbelief, sanctification, saint*) for all students to see throughout the lesson. Read the words to the students, and ask them to signal when they hear the word in the lesson for the first time by standing up. When you come to each word in the lesson, explain the meaning of the word as it relates in the context of the lesson, asking students to share any prior knowledge and then sit down again.

Refer briefly to Poster A. Note the time that has passed between the birth of Ishmael and God's announcement of Isaac's birth, about thirteen years.

Have students turn in their Bibles to Genesis 18:1–19:29. Distribute Lesson Leaflets.

Say Have you ever seen the game show Jeopardy? Today, we're going to do a Jeopardy-type activity to study our Bible story. The answers are in your Lesson Leaflet on pages 2 and 3. You will need to think of the question for that answer. We'll use our Bibles and the Bible Review Cards for this lesson to check our responses. You may all help one another and agree on the question. Raise your hands when you're ready to give the question. Then, you will all write the question in your Lesson Leaflet as I write it on the board.

Say Answer number one is "Three men, one of whom was the Lord." What is the question? Read Genesis 18:1–2. (Who appeared to Abraham by the oaks of Mamre [MAM ray]? Bible Review Card [BRC] 49, question 1) **This is one of the verses in the Old Testament where God appears to His people. God is appearing as a man. Does this remind you of anyone else in the Bible? (Jesus) Yes, Jesus. Many times in the Old Testament, God's people got little peeks into God's plan of salvation through Christ, but not everything was revealed until Jesus came to earth as a man, died on the cross for our sins, and rose from the dead.**

Ask Answer number two is "He offered them food, drink, and rest." What is the question? (What was Abraham's response to his visitors? BRC 50, question 1) **Abraham's response of hospitality was typical for his time, though it may seem unfamiliar to us. Let's see how he showed hospitality to his guests.** Ask students to read verses 6–8. Abraham asked Sarah to make cakes for the visitors, and Abraham also gave them curds and milk and calf meat. You might wish to bring in some fresh cheese curds or cottage cheese to show and share.

Ask Answer number three is "She would have a son." What is the question? (What was the visitors' promise to Sarah? BRC 51, question 1) Have the students read verses 12–13. When Sarah heard the promise that was given to her, she laughed.

Ask Answer number four is "He said that nothing was too hard for the Lord." What is the question? (What did the Lord say to Abraham? BRC 52, question 1) Read Genesis 18:14. **The Lord and the two angels told Sarah, through Abraham, that she would have a son. It would have seemed impossible because of Sarah's age. Once women get beyond a certain age, their bodies are no longer able to bear children. In spite of God's promise to Abraham**

Teacher Tip

If you have reluctant readers or if students have difficulty finding Bible passages, consider marking the verses in a Bible with bookmarks before class, or encourage students to help one another look up the verses.

Key Point

God came to Abraham with the promise of a son. Abraham's descendant, our Lord Jesus, comes to us in Word and Sacraments, telling us that in Him all things are possible.

A Great Idea!

and Sarah, many years had passed and Sarah must have given up on God's promise. How do we know that this is the case? (Sarah laughed.) **Her laughter here was a sign of unbelief. To Sarah, God's promise seemed laughable.**

Because God is omniscient, He knew Sarah's thoughts and was displeased by her lack of faith in the promise He had just made. By asking the question—Why did Sarah laugh?—He was revealing who He was and that He knows all things. Discuss the Faith Word Card *omniscient*. **When Sarah denied the fact that she laughed in disbelief to the message, the Lord confronted her with her sin. He did not do this to shame her, but rather to reveal her sin of unbelief so that she would turn from it to faith in God's promises.** Refer to the Faith Word Card *unbelief*. **Even though Sarah did not believe in God's promise, and even though she denied her sin, God still promised that she would have a son. God is merciful, even when she doubted and denied her sin.**

Children in Bible Times

If time permits, and if it will not break the focus of the students on the Bible study, do the Bible Discovery Guide research at this point. Otherwise, it can be a culminating activity.

Say **Let's look at page 15 of the Bible Discovery Guide to get a little insight into what Sarah would have experienced as a wife with no children. We'll also see how children in ancient Bible times would have lived and what was expected of them.**

Have the students answer these questions:

1. Who were three women in the Bible who had trouble having children? (Sarah, Rachel, Hannah)
2. What are "swaddling clothes"? (Strips of cloth used to tightly wrap an infant)
3. Who were the first teachers of children in that society? (Mothers)
4. What were the girls taught to do? (Become good wives and mothers; learn a variety of household tasks)
5. What were boys taught to do? (Learn a trade, often the same as their fathers; learn to read and write)

Have students complete the cryptogram on page 2 of the Lesson Leaflet before moving to the next event in the story of Abraham and the visitors from heaven and completing the rest of the answers/questions activity. When all students have completed the cryptogram, read the Bible Words together.

Say **"With God all things are possible"** (Matthew 19:26). **Let's look at the verses right before this verse in Matthew.** Have students read Matthew 19:23–25. **What question is Jesus answering when He says, "With God all things are possible"?** (Who then can be saved?) **Not only can God give Sarah a baby in her old age, but also and even more important, God is the one who saves us. And Sarah's baby, Isaac, was part of the family that made God's salvation for all people possible. He was in the family line of Jesus (as we've seen in our Bible Discovery Guide on page 3), through whom we have forgiveness of our sins. That forgiveness is given to us through God's Word, through the water of Baptism, and through the bread and wine, Jesus' body and blood, in the Lord's Supper.**

Now we will continue studying in Genesis 18 and 19 to see another example of God's love for His chosen people. He saved them from destruction, both of body and soul.

Read Genesis 18:16–21. God was showing Abraham and all generations that He hates unbelief and must punish it, but He always carries out His judgments in such a way that He delivers His faithful people. He gives Abraham an opportunity to plead mercy for his nephew Lot and Lot's family.

Ask Answer number five is "He asked six times." What is the question? Read Genesis 18:22–33. Encourage children to count as they listen. (How many times did Abraham ask God to spare Sodom? BRC 53, question 3) **Abraham's prayer was based on mercy, not merit. It is only God's grace that saves us from being destroyed by our sin. Abraham's prayer was unselfish and bold. Did God answer Abraham's prayer?** Allow for responses.

Ask Answer number six is "God hates sin and has to destroy it." What is the question? (Why was God going to destroy Sodom? BRC 54, question 1) If they need help, reread Genesis 18:20, 23–25. **The people in the city were sinful and wicked. They had no regard for the true God.** Refer briefly to Poster B for the places mentioned in these texts—Sodom, Gomorrah, Zoar, and the hills.

Ask Answer number seven is "Two angels." What is the question? (Who rescued Lot and his family? BRC 55, question 2) Read Genesis 19:12–22 to the students, explaining if necessary. **Did God answer Abraham's prayer?** (Yes, and God did more than He promised Abraham. Even though there were not even ten believers in the city, God saved Lot and his family. He also granted Lot's request to flee to Zoar instead of the hills.)

Ask Answer number eight is "The Lord rained sulfur and fire down from heaven." What is the question? Read Genesis 19:23–29. (How did God destroy Sodom? BRC 56, question 1) **What happened to Lot's wife? Why?** (She looked back and became a pillar of salt. She despised God's warning and disobeyed Him.)

Thy Kingdom Come

Have students find the Second Petition of the Lord's Prayer on page 3 of the Lesson Leaflet. Read the petition and its meaning.

Say We read "so that by His grace we believe His holy Word." **God wants us to trust His Word, but like Sarah, we doubt it and think He cannot do what He says. But the good news is that God is faithful and His Word is true. In Christ, all of God's promises are true. Because God hates sin and must punish sinners, we are in need of God's grace. But God is "gracious and merciful, slow to anger and abounding in steadfast love"** (Psalm 145:8). **God saved us from destruction, of both body and soul, by punishing His own Son for our sins. Jesus' suffering and death destroyed sin completely. God's kingdom is ours through Baptism when God gives us the Holy Spirit to believe in Him. Our sin was drowned when we were baptized into Jesus' death. We can rejoice that we have been forgiven.**

Key Point

God came to Abraham with the promise of a son. Abraham's descendant, our Lord Jesus, comes to us in Word and Sacraments, telling us that in Him all things are possible.

Lesson 7

Key Point
God came to Abraham with the promise of a son. Abraham's descendant, our Lord Jesus, comes to us in Word and Sacraments, telling us that in Him all things are possible.

Continue In our sin, we fear God and want to hide our sin from Him, just like Sarah denied that she laughed in disbelief. But since Jesus faced God with the truth of our sin and satisfied God's wrath on the cross, we have nothing to fear and nothing to hide. That's great news!

Thinking about Faith

Introduce Can you think of a word that means "belief in Christ for the forgiveness of sins, life, salvation, and all that we need"? (Faith)

Direct the students' attention to page 3 of the leaflet. Partner the students or work together as a class to complete the activity. Responses to the questions are (1) faith; (2) being sure of what we hope for, and certain of what we do not see; (3) it is a gift of the Spirit; (4) everything; (5) any amount is enough, even as small as a mustard seed; and (6) by faith in the Son of God.

Direct the students to the Faith Words you have displayed.

Ask Which word means "all that the Holy Spirit does through the Word and Sacraments to make us holy"? (Sanctification) Which word names "a faithful believer in Jesus Christ, either living or already in heaven"? (Saint) Sanctification—the making of saints—is the work of the Holy Spirit, who gives us faith. We are made holy through faith in Jesus' death and resurrection. God gives us faith to trust Him. We have been sanctified. God now counts us as righteous. Although we are sinners, we are also saints who have the promise of life eternal in heaven with Jesus some day.

Genesis Word Search

Distribute copies of Reproducible Page 7, found at the end of this lesson, and allow students to complete the word search until Closing.

 Closing (5 minutes)

Teacher Tip
Whether your students have special needs or not, all children need to be reassured that their spiritual growth is more important than academics in a Sunday School setting. Be sure to emphasize to your students that Sunday School is a time to learn more about God and His Word and to grow in a relationship with Him.

Say Let's read our Bible Words on the back of your leaflet. Read Matthew 19:26 together. **How can these words help you when you have doubts about God taking care of you? when you face some difficult times at school with bullies? when your parents or siblings argue? when you have a difficult homework assignment to complete?** Allow for discussion. **God can be trusted. He keeps His word, even when we doubt Him. He forgives us when we sin. He promises to be with us and guide us. We have a gracious and merciful God!**

Sing "If God Himself Be for Me" (*LSB* 724; CD 4) and Luther's Morning Prayer (CD 21).

Say God promised Sarah and Abraham that they would receive the gift of a baby. What a blessing! But babies can be hard work! This week, think about adding a package of wipes or diapers to your grocery list. Whatever we collect next week, we can donate to a place that helps young families take care of their babies.

Pray Dear heavenly Father, You are always quick to give blessings and to show mercy to Your children. Thank You for the blessing of faith, which You freely give to us in grace. Thank You for forgiving us when we doubt Your Word. Please remind us of Your love for us in Jesus and help us share the good news of Jesus' love with others this week. In Jesus' name we pray. Amen.

Abraham's Visitors from Heaven
Genesis 18:1–15; 21:1–7

A Genesis Word Search

Circle or highlight the words that relate to the text from Genesis.

```
N  M  M  H  A  R  A  S  A  T
A  R  A  E  V  E  I  L  E  B
A  I  L  H  R  S  C  C  S  T
N  G  X  O  A  C  A  G  R  S
A  H  R  A  R  R  Y  O  U  U
C  T  C  Y  G  D  B  D  C  R
D  E  S  C  E  N  D  A  N  T
E  O  G  N  I  S  S  E  L  B
H  U  F  A  I  T  H  O  P  E
T  S  W  O  R  S  H  I  P  M
```

ABRAHAM
BELIEVE
BLESSING
CANAAN
CURSE
DESCENDANT
FAITH
GOD
GRACE
HOPE
ISAAC
LORD
MERCY
RIGHTEOUS
SARAH
TRUST
WORSHIP

UPPER ELEMENTARY

Preparing the Lesson

Abraham and Isaac

Genesis 21:1–7; 22:1–19

Lesson 8

Date of Use

Key Point

God provided a ram as a sacrifice for Abraham and Isaac. He provides the perfect sacrifice for our sin: His Son, Jesus, the Lamb of God.

Law/Gospel

God requires a payment for my sin. **God sent His own Son, Jesus, to be sacrificed in payment for my sin.**

Context

God's wonderful promises to Abraham in Genesis 12, including that He would make Abraham into a great nation (v. 2) and that in him all the families of the earth would be blessed (v. 3), hinge on Abraham having a son. Moreover, God said that this son would be borne by Abraham's wife, Sarah (17:19). Twenty-five years after God first made His promises, Abraham and Sarah (who is well past childbearing years) still have no son.

Commentary

The Lord visits Sarah; that is, He draws near to her in grace and miraculously enlivens her dead womb, enabling her to conceive and bear a son. Abraham obeys God's commands regarding the child by naming him Isaac (in fulfillment of Genesis 17:19) and by circumcising him when he is eight days old (in fulfillment of 17:10–13). Isaac's name, which means "he laughs," evokes the laughter of joy at the birth of the miraculous child. Luther says this about the basis of Abraham's joy: "What thus far has been an object of hope, and what he has believed, this is now a reality; . . . the promise has now been made flesh" (Luther's Works 4:4).

Abraham dearly loves his child of the promise. Does he, perhaps, love him more than he loves God? God tests Abraham's love by commanding him to offer Isaac as a burnt offering. Abraham immediately prepares to carry out God's command. But then how will God fulfill His promise that through Isaac Abraham would have many descendants (Genesis 21:12)? God enables Abraham to trust that He will indeed fulfill His promise even if Isaac is sacrificed: Abraham "considered that God was able even to raise [Isaac] from the dead" (Hebrews 11:19).

Abraham and Isaac arrive at the place of sacrifice. It is called Moriah, the place where Abraham's descendant King David will one day build an altar at God's command (1 Chronicles 21:18–28). It is also the site where the city of Jerusalem will one day be founded and where Solomon's temple will be built (2 Chronicles 3:1).

At Moriah, Abraham prepares the altar, binds his son in the manner of an animal sacrifice, and raises the knife to slay him. But the Angel of the Lord (actually a manifestation of God Himself) calls to Abraham from heaven, telling him not to lay a hand on the boy: "For now I know that you fear God, seeing you have not withheld your son, your only son, from Me" (Genesis 22:12).

Abraham lifts his eyes and sees a ram. As Abraham had earlier assured Isaac (22:8), God provided the sacrifice, and Abraham offers it up in place of his son. Again, the Lord calls to Abraham, confirming His earlier promises. Through Abraham's offspring, all the nations of the earth would be blessed. God fulfilled that promise by sending the Savior of the world of sinners, Jesus, from the line of Abraham (Matthew 1:1).

As Abraham laid the wood of the burnt offering on his only son, whom he loved, so God willingly laid the wood of the cross on His only Son, whom He loved. But unlike Isaac, for whom God provided a substitute, Jesus was sacrificed. He is "the Lamb of God, who takes away the sin of the world!" (John 1:29).

To hear an in-depth discussion of this Bible account, visit cph.org/podcast and listen to our Seeds of Faith podcast each week.

Lesson 8

Abraham and Isaac
Genesis 21:1–7; 22:1–19

Connections

Bible Words
The next day [John] saw Jesus coming toward him, and said, "Behold, the Lamb of God, who takes away the sin of the world!" John 1:29

Faith Words
sacrifice, atone/atonement, belief, justify

Hymn
God's Own Child, I Gladly Say It (*LSB* 594:1, 5; CD 2)

Catechism
First Commandment
Apostles' Creed: Second Article

Liturgy
Agnus Dei

Prepare

Create a simple obstacle course in your classroom using chairs, desks, books, and the like. If space or time does not allow the creation of an obstacle course, create two or three simple mazes on paper using two parallel lines about a half-inch apart running in a zigzag pattern from top to bottom. Volunteers will complete the "obstacle course" while blindfolded using a pencil or marker, but still guided by the teacher's instructions.

Have copies of Reproducible Page 8, found at the end of this lesson, and crayons or markers available. All students may enjoy having an opportunity to walk through the obstacle course before the Invocation and opening prayer. Be prepared to spend a few minutes after the lesson for students who may ask to walk through it blindfolded.

1 Opening (5 minutes)

Begin with the Invocation when all of the students have arrived. Make the sign of the cross as you do so.

Say In the name of the Father and of the Son and of the Holy Spirit. Amen.

Sing the hymn "God's Own Child, I Gladly Say It" (*LSB* 594:1, 5; CD 2). Then lead the students in an opening prayer.

Pray Dear heavenly Father, we thank You for bringing us together again today to worship You, to hear Your Word, and to see You in Your

MATERIALS NEEDED

1 Opening

Teacher Tools
CD

Other Supplies
Reproducible Page 8 (TG)
Chairs, desks, books, etc. to use as obstacles (optional)
Blindfold (optional)
Mazes (optional)

2 God Speaks

Teacher Tools
Faith Word Cards 29–32
Posters A and B

3 We Live

Teacher Tools
CD
Faith Word Cards 29–32
Bible Review Cards 1–64
Poster C (optional)

Student Stuff
Lesson Leaflets

Other Supplies
Resource Pages 2, 6–8 (TG; optional)

4 Closing

Teacher Tools
CD

Student Stuff
Lesson Leaflets

Other Supplies
Blindfold; chairs, desks, books, etc. to use as obstacles (optional)
Reproducible Page 8 (TG)
Poster board

Lesson 8

Sacraments. We ask You to be with us as we study Your Word; send Your Holy Spirit to increase our faith. We pray in Jesus' name. Amen.

Obstacles

Ask for a volunteer to walk through the obstacle course, possibly a child who hasn't had an opportunity. (See the notes for a tabletop alternative under "Prepare" at the beginning of this lesson.)

Say It looked like it was pretty simple for (student's name) **to get through the obstacle course. Let's see if it's that easy blindfolded.**

Ask for another volunteer to be blindfolded and to walk the course. Guide the student with simple commands, such as "three steps forward, one to your right," and so on. Ask for a third volunteer, and blindfold the student.

Say (Child's name), **I'm going to change the obstacle course before you walk through it.** After the student is blindfolded, make minor changes in the obstacles. Provide simple commands to assist the student through the course.

Say **It's easy to follow a path when we can see the way. It gets harder when we can't see the path, or if we don't know where it is. Today's lesson is about a time when God asked Abraham to follow His directions without knowing what might happen.**

2 God Speaks (10 minutes)

God Tests Abraham

Say **We have been reading and studying a number of Bible stories about one of God's saints, Abraham. God has promised a son to be born to Abraham and his wife, Sarah. Although Sarah doubted God, He fulfilled His plan of salvation. Listen as we read about the birth of Abraham's son, Isaac.**

Either read Genesis 21:1–7 to the children or invite several students to take turns reading the verses from their Bibles. Refer to Poster A to indicate the date of Isaac's birth.

Display the Faith Word Cards for this lesson on a chalk tray, or lay them on a table with only the word visible. As you proceed through the lesson, introduce the word by asking "Which word means . . . ?" or "Which word names . . . ?" Then, let a student guess or answer. This can be an easy, active way of engaging the children throughout the lesson.

Ask the students to close their eyes and envision the scenes as you read Genesis 22:1–19 aloud. (Students may have a difficult time keeping their eyes closed. They may put their heads down on the desk or turn their chairs to face the outside of the room with their backs to their classmates.) Then, ask them to open their eyes. Using Poster B, identify the location of Beersheba (BEAR SHE buh) and Moriah (moh RYE uh).

Discuss **Why did God test Abraham?** (God wanted Abraham to be sure that nothing, not even the love of his own child, was more important to him than loving God. Although the Ten Commandments had not yet been given, God, in the First Commandment, commands us to have no other gods before Him.) **What was the test?** (God asked Abraham to sacrifice his son, Isaac, as a burnt offering.)

Teacher Tip
Keep ability and developmental levels in mind when selecting volunteers. Focus on the strengths of each student as they volunteer, and encourage reluctant or infrequent volunteers by choosing them whenever possible.

Key Point
God provided a ram as a sacrifice for Abraham and Isaac. He provides the perfect sacrifice for our sin, His Son, Jesus, the Lamb of God.

Lesson 8

Key Point

God provided a ram as a sacrifice for Abraham and Isaac. He provides the perfect sacrifice for our sin, His Son, Jesus, the Lamb of God.

Ask **Which of our Faith Words means "the offering demanded and provided for by God in payment for sin"?** (Sacrifice) **Why would this sacrifice have been especially difficult for Abraham?** (Isaac was the son promised to Abraham and Sarah in their old age. God promised that Abraham would have many descendants through Isaac.) **What might Abraham have been tempted to do?** Allow for responses. (Abraham might have been tempted not to go to Moriah, to take another offering, or to leave Isaac at home.) **Are we ever tempted to do things contrary to God's will?** (We, too, are tempted; even Jesus was tempted in the flesh. God gives us the faith to trust Him when we are tempted to disobey Him.) **How did Abraham answer Isaac's question about the lamb for the sacrifice?** (God would provide the lamb.) **Who stopped Abraham from actually sacrificing Isaac?** (The Angel of the Lord. The Angel said, "You have not withheld your son *from Me*." **How did Abraham respond when he saw the ram caught in the thicket?** (He worshiped by sacrificing the ram.) **How do you think Abraham and Isaac felt after the entire experience?** Allow for the sharing of ideas. Direct the children to the picture on the front of the Lesson Leaflet to contemplate the emotions of father and son. **What was God's renewed promise to Abraham?** (Abraham would have too many descendants to count, and they would be strong. All nations on earth would be blessed because of Abraham's obedience to God. Lead the students to understand that Abraham's most important descendant would be Jesus, God's own Son.)

3 We Live (20 minutes)

God Provides the Sacrifice

Have the children read together the Bible Words on page 4 of the leaflet. Make copies of Bible Words Puzzle 8 for students to complete now or at home.

Say **Which Faith Word means "satisfaction or payment required by the Law on account of our sin"?** (atone/atonement)

Before class, place bookmarks in two or more Bibles at the passages in the Lesson Leaflet activities. Ask volunteers to read a premarked passage; then, answer the question as a group. Or place several Bibles on the table, each open to one of the verses and numbered accordingly. This will speed up this activity.

Help the students understand the difference between Law and Gospel.

Explain **Let's look at the top of page 2 in your leaflet.** Ask a student to read the paragraph above the first illustration. **To be saved under the Law required that God's people keep His commandments perfectly. Since no one can keep the Law perfectly, God required Old Testament believers to offer sacrifices to atone for their sins. Scripture outlined details of the sacrifices God required. The sacrifice in this account is a blood sacrifice, which indicated a complete commitment to God. Such sacrifices foreshadowed the once-for-all sacrifice that Jesus would make on humankind's behalf on the cross.**

Ask a student to read the paragraph that accompanies the cross illustration.

Ask **Which Faith Word means "to declare free from blame"?** (justify) **Which one means "something one holds to be true or real"?** (belief)

Say **In contrast to the Law, under the Gospel and through God's grace, He sent His own Son, Jesus Christ, to *justify* us, that is, to keep the Law per-**

fectly and to die for the sins of mankind. Jesus was the perfect, final sacrifice to atone for sins. We sin when we think there is anything we can do for ourselves to remove or pay for our sins instead of what Christ has done for us. Through faith in Christ, our *belief* **that Jesus died for us, we have forgiveness of our sins and eternal salvation.**

Ask What are some things people think they can do to please God and pay for their sins? Allow for responses. **Have you ever had this thought that you could do something to pay (atone) for your sins and please God?** Point out that religions that require a person to do something for God in order to receive His blessings are false religions. Discuss God's patience and forgiveness.

The Lamb of God

Direct the students' attention to the bottom of page 2 in the Lesson Leaflet. (Lyrics are also available on the CD.) Ask a volunteer to read the directions. You may play the hymn softly in the background as students work independently, or play one stanza at a time, pause the recording to read the Scripture, and work through the activity as a class. Responses are Stanza 1—God, Lamb; Stanza 2—Lamb, God, sins; Stanza 3—redeems; Stanza 4—sin, righteousness; and Stanza 5—Thanks, disciples; Refrain—Worthy, Lamb.

Provide copies of the Second Article of the Apostles' Creed found on Resource Page 2 (or use Poster C), and read it together. Especially focus on the second paragraph in the explanation: "who has redeemed me, a lost and condemned person, purchased and won me from all sins, from death, and from the power of the devil; not with gold or silver, but with His holy, precious blood and with His innocent suffering and death." Have the children relate the hymn to the Second Article, pointing out phrases in each that correspond. Sing the hymn together.

God's Promises to Me

Direct the students' attention to page 3 of the Lesson Leaflet. As each statement is read aloud, do a quick visual check of their responses by asking them to show a thumbs-up or thumbs-down response in front of their chest. Allow time for the students to draw a cross shape around each one that is true before you proceed to reading the next statement. Discuss any statements, but especially those that do not correctly reflect God's Word.

1. When I don't trust God, it's no big deal. God doesn't really care. **What is wrong with this statement?** (God wants me to believe and trust in Him.)

2. Faith is trusting in God's promises. **True**

3. I do not trust God, but He gives me faith to trust Him. **True**

4. In my sin, I doubt God's promises. **True**

5. I will go to heaven because of the good works I do. **What is wrong with saying that I will go to heaven because of the good works I do?** (Because I am sinful, the good works I do are unacceptable in God's sight; "all our righteous deeds are like a polluted garment" [Isaiah 64:6]. I will go to heaven because of Jesus' good work on the cross for me. Because of Jesus' good work, God now sees my efforts as good too.)

6. God grants me faith in Jesus, my Savior. **True**

7. God doesn't keep His promises. **How do we know this is not correct?** (In

Lesson 8

Key Point
God provided a ram as a sacrifice for Abraham and Isaac. He provides the perfect sacrifice for our sin, His Son, Jesus, the Lamb of God.

the story of Abraham, we see how God kept His promises to give Abraham a son. He also preserves Isaac by providing the ram for the sacrifice He desired. Later, God provides another sacrifice, His Son, Jesus. Through Him, God keeps His promises to forgive us when we sin. We were marked in Baptism with the sign of the cross.)

8. Faith is a gift of God. **True**

9. I trust in God all the time. **Why is this statement incorrect?** (Though Abraham showed remarkable faith in the face of God's command to sacrifice his son, I at times doubt that God can do what He promises. I do not trust God. God mercifully carries out His promise to forgive me, thus giving me reason to trust Him in all things.)

10. God wants me to believe in Him. **True**

Review

If time permits, review the lesson by playing one of the Bible Review Games (Resource Pages 6–8 in the back of this guide), using the Bible Review Cards for this and previous lessons.

4 Closing (12 minutes)

The Lord Will Provide

Ask for one final volunteer to be blindfolded. Before he or she begins the obstacle course, ask him or her to wait a moment as you change the obstacles again. While the student is blindfolded, remove all of the obstacles. (For the table-top alternative, use a blank piece of paper.) Give simple commands as if there were obstacles. After they have completed the "course," show the student that there were no obstacles.

Say **God doesn't always take away our obstacles. He doesn't promise that we won't have difficult times. But He provides the faith we need to trust Him to lead us. And that is better than no obstacles at all.**

Direct the students to the final section of the Lesson Leaflet. Invite the students to consider how God's promise to provide for them can give them confidence in difficult times. Invite them to write prayers of thanksgiving. Consider recording them on a poster board to share with hallway passersby.

If the students have time, allow them to complete Reproducible Page 8. Focus on today's Bible Words at the bottom of the page and also on page 4 of the Lesson Leaflet. John knew that this was the final, perfect sacrifice for the sins of all people.

Invite the students to chant the Agnus Dei while coloring their design. It is found in *Lutheran Service Book* on page 163. Or sing again the hymn "God's Own Child, I Gladly Say It" (*LSB* 594:1, 5; CD 2).

Conclude by allowing volunteers to share the prayers they have written. Include this prayer.

Pray **We thank You, heavenly Father, for loving us and guiding us through each day. Forgive us when our faith is weak. Give us faith like Abraham's, that we may follow Your will without being afraid. Thank You for providing Your Son as the sacrifice for our sins. In Jesus' name we pray. Amen.**

Faith in Action

Liturgy Link
Worshipers chant the Agnus Dei prior to the distribution of Holy Communion. We are singing to the Lamb of God present on the altar with His very body and very blood sacrificed—given and shed—for the forgiveness of sins.

The Lamb of God—Agnus Dei

Color the spaces according to the following key: "Y"=Yellow; "R"=Red; "B"=Blue; "G"=Green; "K"=Black; "W"=White.

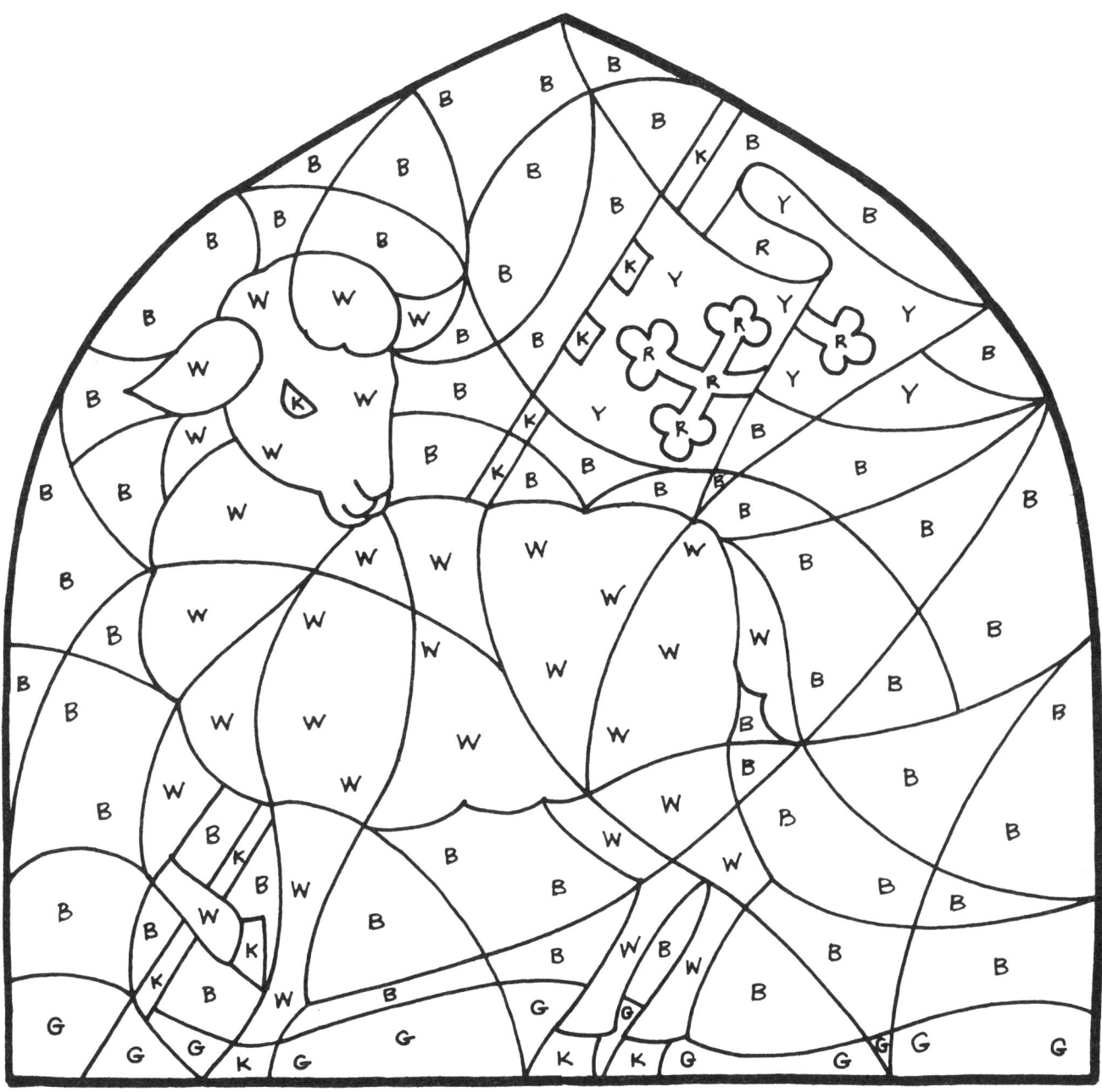

The next day [John] saw Jesus coming toward him, and said, "Behold, the Lamb of God, who takes away the sin of the world!"

John 1:29

UPPER ELEMENTARY

Preparing the Lesson

Isaac and Rebekah
Genesis 24

Lesson 9

_____
Date of Use

Key Point
God worked His plan of salvation through the lives of Isaac and Rebekah. God's plan for our salvation is fulfilled through Jesus, their descendant.

Law/Gospel
God wants me to trust Him for all that I need. **God provides all that I need and gives me forgiveness, life, and salvation through His Son.**

Context
Abraham and his family, including Isaac, the son of promise, continue to live among the pagan people in the land of Canaan. Abraham, not wanting Isaac to marry one of the Canaanites, charges his oldest servant, unnamed but perhaps Eliezer, to seek a godly wife for Isaac among Abraham's kindred in Mesopotamia.

Commentary
Abraham entrusts the search for a godly wife for Isaac to a trusted servant. He makes the servant swear not to take a wife for Isaac from the Canaanites. Instead, Abraham sends the servant to bring a wife from the house of Abraham's kindred. The servant wonders whether he should take Isaac back there if the woman will not consent to come back with him.

The faith of Abraham shines forth as he assures the servant that God will send His angel before the servant, making his mission successful. But Abraham knows that even if the woman is not willing to come, Isaac must not leave the land to which God has called Abraham.

The servant departs for the northern region of Mesopotamia, the area around Haran, where Abraham's family first settled after they left Ur of the Chaldeans (Genesis 11:31). The servant bears gifts for the prospective bride and her family, testimonies to the abundant way God has blessed Abraham. The servant asks God to "show steadfast love" (24:12) to Abraham by guiding the servant to the woman He has chosen for Isaac. Before the servant finishes praying, God wonderfully answers the prayer by the appearance of Rebekah, the daughter of Bethuel and granddaughter of Nahor, Abraham's brother. God's abundant grace is further evidenced because Rebekah is also beautiful, a virgin, and very hospitable.

The servant is welcomed into Rebekah's home by her brother Laban with the greeting, "Come in, O blessed of the Lord" (24:31), a greeting that gives testimony to his faith in the Lord. The servant describes how God has blessed his master with great wealth and a son in his old age. He details how the Lord has guided his journey to Rebekah, the one he believes God has chosen to be Isaac's wife.

Rebekah's father and brother agree that indeed "the thing has come from the Lord" (v. 50). Rebekah herself agrees to accompany the servant without delay.

Upon the servant's return, Isaac takes Rebekah to be his wife, and he loves her. From their descendants would be born the Christ, the Bridegroom of the Church. For His Bride, Christ would give His life and cleanse her with the waters of Holy Baptism (Ephesians 5:25–27).

To hear an in-depth discussion of this Bible account, visit cph.org/podcast and listen to our Seeds of Faith podcast each week.

Lesson 9

Isaac and Rebekah

Genesis 24

Connections

Bible Words
The eyes of all look to You, and You give them their food in due season. You open Your hand; You satisfy the desire of every living thing. Psalm 145:15–16 (CD 9)

Faith Words
Law, Gospel, grace, iniquity

Hymn
Praise God from Whom All Blessings Flow (*LSB* 805; CD 5)

Catechism
Apostles' Creed: First Article
Sixth Commandment
Lord's Prayer: Fourth Petition

5, 16–20

1 Opening (7 minutes)

Take advantage of unplanned moments to reinforce teaching. Play the catechism songs or hymns as background music during arrival time. Make review games available for students who arrive early. Begin with the Invocation.

Say In the name of the Father and of the Son and of the Holy Spirit. Amen.

Play and sing the hymn "Praise God from Whom All Blessings Flow" (*LSB* 805; CD 5). After singing the hymn,

Ask What are some of the "countless gifts of love" that God gives you (st. 1)? Allow for responses. Direct the students to the First Article of the Apostles' Creed and the explanation in their Lesson Leaflets on page 3. Sing along with the catechism songs (CD 16–20). Make a list on the board of all the blessings listed in the First Article that God provides for us (house, home, body, soul, food, clothing, all I have, etc.). **Does God also provide parents, brothers, sisters, and other relatives? Does God provide husbands and wives? Will He provide a wife for you, boys, or a husband for you, girls?** Expect and allow for a little lighthearted discussion.

Pray Dear Lord, You always provide all that we need. Help us to be grateful for Your blessings and to never take for granted Your many gifts. Thank You for our families, for our homes, for clothing, shoes, food, drink, and all material things You give us. Most especially, we thank You for Jesus' death on the cross for our salvation. Through Christ, we pray. Amen.

MATERIALS NEEDED

1 Opening	2 God Speaks	3 We Live	4 Closing
Teacher Tools	**Teacher Tools**	**Teacher Tools**	**Teacher Tools**
CD	Faith Word Cards 33–36	CD	CD
	Poster B		
Student Stuff	**Student Stuff**	**Student Stuff**	**Student Stuff**
Lesson Leaflets	Bible Discovery Guide	Lesson Leaflets	Lesson Leaflets
	Lesson Leaflets		
	Other Supplies	**Other Supplies**	
	Wedding photos	Reproducible Page 9 (TG)	
		Cardstock	
		Contact paper (optional)	
		Cardboard or wooden craft sticks (optional)	

Lesson 9

2 God Speaks (20 minutes)

God's Plan for Isaac

To introduce the Bible story, bring in a few photographs of a wedding, yours or someone else's. Let the children look at them and talk about weddings they have been to.

Say We're going to see now how God provided a wife for Isaac. Does anyone know her name? Let's begin by looking at the Bible Discovery Guide to learn a little about marriage in the days of Abraham. Have the students read page 14 in the Bible Discovery Guide.

Discuss What surprised you about marriage in Bible times? Answers will vary. Some might include the young age at which people married and the fact that all marriages were arranged. **In the past, although young men or women may have been able to express their desire to marry a certain person, the parents of the children still arranged the marriages. What do you think about that?**

Genesis 24 is a long chapter. It may be helpful for you to do most of the reading or to have students read the passages aloud, taking turns reading verses. Break up the chapter into the following segments.

Say **Open your Bibles to Genesis 24. Let's read verses 1–9.** Have students take turns, each reading a verse. **Look at verses 2–4. Whom did Abraham ask to help him?** (His servant, the oldest in his household) **What did Abraham ask the servant to do?** (Find a wife for Isaac from their own land) Abraham's faith again is evident because he trusts that God will make the servant's mission successful. **Abraham was concerned that if Isaac married a wife from Canaan, where people worshiped many gods, he might be tempted to turn his back on the one true God.** They lived in a heathen land. In verses 6–8, notice the strong insistence upon the promise God had given to Abraham. See also Deuteronomy 7:3 and 2 Corinthians 6:14, where God also speaks about the importance of choosing a spouse who is a believer in Jesus Christ. It may be helpful to instill some of these godly ideas in your students' minds.

Read verses 10–14, or have students read the passage.

Discuss **Where did the servant go?** (To Mesopotamia, Abraham's homeland) Show students on Poster B the location of Mesopotamia [mess oh poh TAME ih uh] near Ur. **What did the servant ask God for?** (He prayed that God would lead him to the right wife for Isaac. He asked God specifically for a woman to offer to get a drink not only for him but also for his camels as a sign of God's steadfast love for Abraham.)

Read verses 15–28. After reading the passage, ask for a volunteer to reread verse 15. Point out that God answers the servant's prayer even before he finishes speaking.

Say **God is so gracious that He provides for the servant even before he has completed his request. This is also how God listens to us. How does the servant know that Rebekah is the one that God has chosen for Isaac?** (She

Key Point

God worked His plan of salvation through the lives of Isaac and Rebekah. God's plan for our salvation is fulfilled through Jesus, their descendant.

Lesson 9

Key Point

God worked His plan of salvation through the lives of Isaac and Rebekah. God's plan for our salvation is fulfilled through Jesus, their descendant.

not only gives water to him but also offers to water the camels, exactly answering the servant's prayer.) **Whose family is Rebekah from?** See verses 15 and 24, if necessary. (Bethuel [beh THOO ell], the son of Milcah [MILL kuh], the wife of Nahor [NAY hor] who is Abraham's brother and Isaac's uncle) **This is significant because the servant then knows that this woman is from the family of Abraham.**

Read verses 29–33, especially focusing on verse 31. Rebekah's brother, Laban [LAY bihn], welcomed the servant into their home, and this greeting helps us know that he believes in the Lord.

Say In verses 34–48, Abraham's servant describes to Rebekah's father and brother how he met Rebekah and tells them that he wants to take her to Isaac to be his wife. Remember from the Bible Discovery Guide that her family would have arranged Rebekah's marriage.

Read verses 49–61.

Ask What was the request from Rebekah's father and brother? (That she remain with them for ten days) **They agreed with the servant to ask Rebekah what she thought about staying or leaving with him. What was her response?** ("I will go," v. 58.) **God provided a wife from Abraham's homeland and also helped her to be willing to travel immediately to meet her new husband.**

Read verses 62–67.

Ask What happens in the last portion of this chapter? (Isaac and Rebekah meet, and Rebekah becomes Isaac's wife.)

Symbols of Love

Direct students to the top of page 2 in the Lesson Leaflet. Ask a volunteer to read the first paragraph.

Ask What do brides and grooms usually give each other when they marry to symbolize their love for each other? (A ring) Isaac gave Rebekah a ring, which she wore in her nose. See verse 47 again.

Ask another volunteer to read the second paragraph from the leaflet. Be sensitive to any students that may have divorced parents. Remind them that, like all our sins, unfaithfulness in marriage and separation through divorce are sins Jesus paid for when He died on the cross.

Ask What symbol do we have from the Bridegroom of the Church, Jesus, that shows us how much He loves us? (A cross) **Isaac loved Rebekah. Think of how much more God loved the world, so much that He gave His only Son, the descendant of Isaac and Rebekah, to be our Savior from sin, death, and the devil.**

This would be a good time to briefly use the Faith Word Cards for this lesson. Have students read the word. Then flip the card and have them read the definition. Let students come forward to write comments or draw visuals, such as these:

Law—this can refer to the Ten Commandments, but also includes all parts of Scripture that tell us what God expects us to do. The Law shows us our sin and the need for a Savior. Visuals could include the acronym S-O-S (show our sin) or the two stone tablets of the Law.

Gospel—write GOSPEL vertically on the left side of the board. After each letter, write a phrase of John 3:16 (Gospel in a nutshell) in this manner:

> **G**od so loved the world that He gave His
> **O**ne and only
> **S**on, that whoever believes in Him shall not
> **P**erish, but have
> **E**ternal
> **L**ife.

Grace—write GRACE vertically on the other side of the board. After each letter, add the message below:

> **G**od's
> **R**iches
> **A**t
> **C**hrist's
> **E**xpense

Iniquity—draw a target with an arrow in a bull's-eye on the board. The target God has set up for us is perfection. Anything less than perfection is sin, or *iniquity*, "missing the mark."

3 We Live (20 minutes)

God's Plan for Me

Ask As you think about all that happened with the servant and Rebekah in Genesis 24, what are four things God provided in this chapter? (Answers may vary. God provided a faithful servant to Abraham. He provided for the exact answer to the servant's prayer. He provided Rebekah for Isaac, who was not only beautiful but also from Abraham's family and his homeland, as Abraham specified. In so doing, God worked His plan of salvation for all people.) **Which is most important for us?** Allow for responses. **God worked His plan of salvation through the lives of Isaac, Rebekah, and their descendants—fulfilling it through Jesus, the descendant of Isaac and Rebekah.**

Say Now, let's think about how God provides for us. On page 2 of your Lesson Leaflet is a rebus, a story told in symbols or pictures. Let's read it aloud. The rebus is the Fourth Petition of the Lord's Prayer—give us this day our daily bread. Continue with the activity that follows the rebus. The only items on the list that are not daily bread are TV, bully, video games, and toys. Some could be disputed, but the answer to the question "What is meant by daily bread?" (written upside down on the leaflet) explains that daily bread includes everything that has to do with the support and needs of the body. **Let's read Psalm 145:15–16 to see what God gives us. These are your Bible Words.** Have students look up the Bible Words in their Bibles or read them from the Lesson Leaflet, page 4. (The Book of Psalms is in the approximate center of the Bible). **Who looks to God for all they need?** (All—"the eyes of all look to You.") **What do we look to God for?** (For "food at the proper time"

Teacher Tip

Instead of always asking questions that require language in the response, consider allowing students with language deficits to point at pictures. As an alternative, you could rephrase questions to elicit a yes or no response.

Lesson 9

and all our "desires") **Is a husband or wife something you desire?** Expect light-hearted comments about marriage and future spouses. **To whom should you look for a husband or wife? What qualities should you look for in a spouse?** Allow for responses. Guide them to understand that just as Abraham trusted God to provide a faithful Christian wife for Isaac, so we can trust God to do the same for us. Encourage children to pray to God, even at their young age in life, for a Christian husband or wife.

Help students memorize the Bible Words by playing and singing the Bible Words song from the CD, track 9. Make copies of Bible Words Puzzle 9 for students to complete now or at home.

Say **God wants us to trust Him to provide all that we need. However, we are sinful and often doubt His care. Despite our lack of trust, God provides all that we need. Even though we sometimes think we are able to take care of ourselves, we cannot care for our own needs.**

Ask **What are some examples or times when you think you can take care of yourself?** Allow for discussion. Some responses might be not needing a babysitter when their parents are gone; being able to stay home alone after school until parents come home from work; being tempted to steal money or possessions in order to have school supplies or snacks; and the like. **When do we doubt God's care?** As the teacher, you may be aware of specific things in your students' lives, thus helping to make this discussion more personal.

Say **The good news is that in spite of our sin, God takes care of us and works through us to accomplish His plan of salvation for us. The Fourth Petition explanation also says that "we pray in this petition that God would lead us to . . . receive our daily bread with thanksgiving."**

Continue **Let's think a little more about the gifts God gives us by thinking about it in a slightly different way. Pretend that a friend of yours loaned you a very important item. Maybe it's a CD or a favorite toy that he or she asked you to take care of. Or maybe your friend went on vacation and you and your parents are helping to take care of the family pet while they are gone. You could be called a caretaker, being responsible for the item that someone left in your care. How would you treat the item that your friend trusts you to care for?** Allow for responses. **Hopefully, you would take good care of it. You wouldn't let the pet run away from your house the minute your friend leaves for vacation. You'd feel terrible if something happened, wouldn't you? This is a picture of the way we care for the things that God gives to us. Our money isn't really ours; it's a gift from God that we use to take care of our needs. Everything we have is a gift from God that He gives to all people to support our body and life. We are caretakers of the gifts God gives us, giving thanks to Him for opening His hand and satisfying our desires.**

Ask **What is the most important thing that God provides for us?** Allow for responses. **The most important thing that God gave us is the gift of salvation in Jesus Christ. Because of Jesus' sacrifice on the cross, God is patient with me and forgives my disobedience for Jesus' sake. Because I am baptized, I know my sin, my iniquity, has been washed away. This is God's grace, His Gospel, at work.**

Key Point
God worked His plan of salvation through the lives of Isaac and Rebekah. God's plan for our salvation is fulfilled through Jesus, their descendant.

Copy Reproducible Page 9, found at the end of this lesson, onto heavy cardstock to make place mats. Provide markers or crayons for the students so they can color their place mat to be used at home. The place mats can be a reminder to give thanks and praise to our God, who provides all we need. If available, use clear contact paper to cover the mat. Listen to the Bible Words song (CD 9) again while the students color their place mats.

Instead of creating a place mat, students may choose to frame the picture with cardboard or wooden craft sticks. This can be a great gift for home-bound members of the congregation.

4 Closing (3 minutes)

Students may complete the maze on page 3 in the leaflet now or at home.

Sing "Praise God from Whom All Blessings Flow" (*LSB* 805; CD 5).

Pray **Dear Father in heaven, who provides everything we need, including the most wonderful gift of salvation through our Lord Jesus, please help us trust in You to care for us and to help us to care for others, always showing the love of Christ in our lives. Through our Lord Jesus Christ we pray. Amen.**

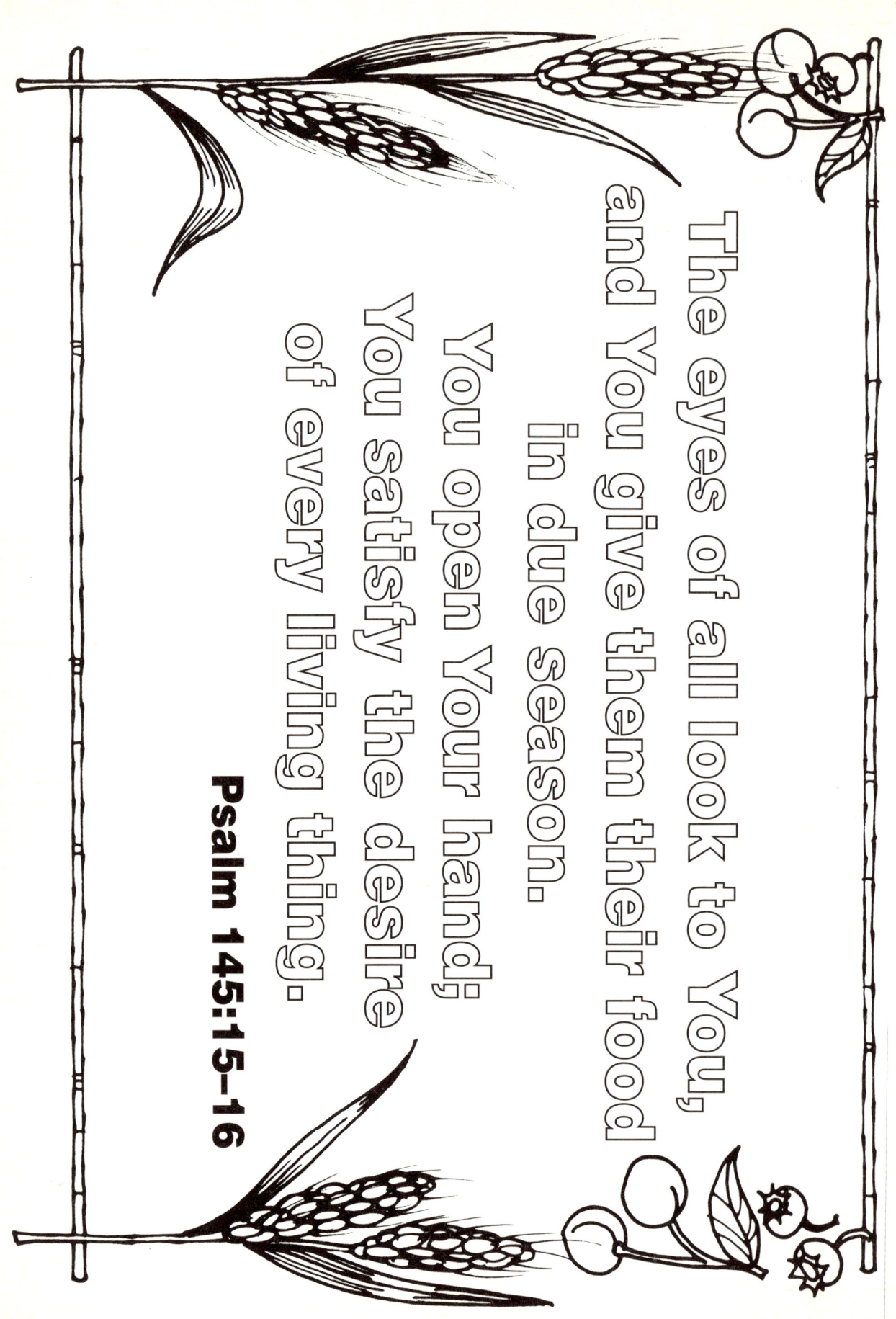

UPPER ELEMENTARY

Preparing the Lesson

Jacob and Esau

Genesis 25:19–34; 27:1–40

Lesson 10

_____
Date of Use

Key Point

God worked through Jacob and Esau, despite their sin, to advance His plan of salvation. In spite of our sinful actions, God accomplishes His will and plan for our lives.

Law/**Gospel**

God does not want me to lie and deceive others, but to trust Him and follow His way. **Because of His Son, Jesus, God forgives all my sins and promises to work all things together for my good.**

Context

Isaac and Rebekah married when Isaac was forty years old. Reminiscent of Abraham and Sarah, almost twenty years later Isaac and Rebekah have no son to be heir of the promise given to Abraham.

Commentary

Isaac prays to the Lord on behalf of his barren wife, and God enables Rebekah to conceive. As Luther says, "This conception is not the result of the flesh or of nature; God wanted it to take place through the prayer of the saintly patriarch" (Luther's Works 4:343). God's superabundant grace gives not just one son, but two. As the babies struggle in her womb, Rebekah asks God what is happening. He tells her, "Two nations are in your womb," and contrary to custom, "the older shall serve the younger" (Genesis 25:23).

Paul quotes this verse in Romans 9:10–12 to illustrate "God's purpose of election." The firstborn son, Esau, grows up to be a hunter and is beloved by his father, while the younger, Jacob, is a quiet, tent-dwelling man who has captured the affection of his mother.

Perhaps thinking that the birthright of the firstborn son will automatically go to him regardless, Esau one day sells his birthright to Jacob for a bowl of lentil stew. The birthright includes a double portion of the inheritance and the position of family head when the father dies.

Before he dies, Isaac wishes to bless his favored son, Esau. He instructs Esau to hunt game and prepare for him a favorite meal. Unwilling to trust God to fulfill in His own time His promise that Esau would serve Jacob, Rebekah and Jacob scheme to have Jacob impersonate Esau so that Isaac will bless Jacob.

While ingenious, the plan threatens to derail when Isaac questions how quickly the hunter found game and cooked it and then recognizes Jacob's voice. Jacob sins further by saying that God was involved in the nonexistent hunt (Genesis 27:20). But God works His own purposes, allowing Isaac to be deceived. Isaac blesses his son Jacob, granting him an abundance of the necessities of this life, a dominant political kingdom and dominion over his brother, and the blessing given to Abraham that those who bless him will be blessed and those who curse him, cursed (12:3a).

Thus Isaac, thinking he is blessing Esau, tries to reverse what God has said about the older serving the younger. But he stops short of passing along the part of the blessing that promises a Messiah through whom all the families of the earth will be blessed (12:3b). Later, in 28:4, Isaac will knowingly pass on to Jacob the entire blessing given to Abraham.

God's blessing through the patriarch, as Luther says, is no mere wish, but it "states facts and is sure to be fulfilled. . . . It is the bestowal of a good thing" (Luther's Works 5:140). It cannot be revoked. Though Esau pleads with tears, his father has only an inferior blessing for him. God's finest blessing, the blessing of Abraham, goes to Jacob. Through Jacob, God would bless the world with the Savior from sin.

To hear an in-depth discussion of this Bible account, visit cph.org/podcast and listen to our Seeds of Faith podcast each week.

Lesson 10
Jacob and Esau
Genesis 25:19–34; 27:1–40

Bible Words
And I am sure of this, that He who began a good work in you will bring it to completion at the day of Jesus Christ. Philippians 1:6 (CD 14)

Faith Words
inheritance, birthright, covet, trust

Hymn
If God Himself Be for Me (*LSB* 724; CD 4)

Catechism
Eighth and Ninth Commandments
Lord's Prayer: Third Petition

Liturgy Link
Aaronic Blessing

Prepare the nametags called for in the Opening activity.

For a unique experience, prepare lentil soup from the recipe provided on Reproducible Page 10, found at the end of this lesson. Have some available for the students to sample before class or during the Bible study.

1 Opening (7 minutes)

Distribute the Faith Word Cards for this lesson to a few students. Ask students to display them when they come up in the lesson.

When all the students have arrived, open with the Invocation. Invite students to make the sign of the cross as you do so. Then begin class with prayer.

Say In the name of the Father and of the Son and of the Holy Spirit. Amen.

Pray Dear heavenly Father, thank You for watching over us and bringing us together today. Send Your Holy Spirit to be among us and to help us understand as we study Your Word. Lead us to know the importance of Your will in our lives and to gladly follow Your ways. In Jesus' name we pray. Amen.

Prepare nametags for each of your students with names of brothers from the Bible (Cain and Abel; Shem [shim], Ham [hamm], and Japheth [JAY fehth]; Isaac and Ishmael; Jacob and Esau; Joseph and Benjamin [other brothers, sons born to Jacob, include Reuben, Simeon, Levi, Judah, Dan, Naphtali, Gad, Asher, Issachar, and Zebulun]; Ephraim and Manasseh; Simon and Andrew; James and John; and others). Sets of names can be repeated, if necessary. Apply the nametags to your students randomly, but use all names in any set of brothers. If necessary, put a nametag on yourself. To begin the lesson, challenge the students to stand and find those other students who are their "brothers." If necessary, invite them to consult a Bible. When all the matches are confirmed, have the students return to their seats.

MATERIALS NEEDED

1 Opening
Teacher Tools
Faith Word Cards 37–40
Other Supplies
Adhesive nametags or paper and masking tape

2 God Speaks
Teacher Tools
Faith Word Cards 37–40
Posters A and B
Student Stuff
Lesson Leaflets
Other Supplies
Lentil soup (optional)

3 We Live
Teacher Tools
CD
Student Stuff
Lesson Leaflets

4 Closing
Teacher Tools
CD
Resource Page 3 (TG; optional)
Other Supplies
Luther's Small Catechism (optional)
Reproducible Page 10 (TG)

Ask Do all brothers get along with one another? (No) **Did the biblical brothers you represent get along?** Answers will vary. **Why don't some brothers get along?** (The specifics the students mention will vary, but the basic answer is our sinful nature.)

Say Today, we will study two of these brothers, sons of Isaac, who did not get along. We'll see how their conflict affected God's plans for His people.

2 God Speaks (20 minutes)

Use Poster A to identify when the story takes place. Point out Canaan and Beersheba on Poster B, where today's story takes place. Direct the students' attention to page 2 of the Lesson Leaflet. Ask them to listen and follow along in their Bibles as you read the story in the following segments. Pause after each segment to allow them to identify and number the appropriate drawing.

Use the numbered drawings to discuss the story.

Drawing 1: Genesis 25:19–28—Jacob and Esau as young men.

Discuss **When Rebekah prayed about her unborn sons, what did God tell her?** (He told her that her twin sons would each lead a great nation and that the oldest son would serve the younger son.) Refer to the Faith Word Card *inheritance*. The tradition of the day made the oldest son the more influential son, the one who would gain the largest portion of his father's inheritance. But God tells Rebekah right away, before they are born, that this would not be the case with her sons. **What are the names of the sons, and which one is older? Which parent favors which son?** (Esau, firstborn, is Isaac's favorite, and Jacob, born second, is Rebekah's favorite child.) Esau means "hairy." Sometimes Esau is known as Edom, which means "red." Jacob means "grasps the heel," which he did at his birth, but it also can mean "trips up" or "deceives." We see this to be true also as the story progresses.

Drawing 2: Genesis 25:29–34—Jacob trading his bowl of stew to Esau, who is dressed from the hunt. Discuss the Faith Word Card *birthright*.

Discuss **How important to Esau is his birthright?** (It is useless. He is willing to sell it for a single meal. He shows a lack of concern for God's promise, or the significance of the birthright.) **Why would the birthright be important for Jacob? Was this how God intended Jacob to obtain the birthright?** (God had promised that Jacob would be greater than Esau. Here, Jacob shows a lack of faith in God's promise by trying to manipulate the situation in his own favor. He is also guilty of coveting, which we know breaks the Ninth Commandment: "You shall not covet.") Discuss *covet* using the Faith Word Card. God forbids every sinful desire to get our neighbor's possessions openly or by trickery. Jacob tricked Isaac into giving him the birthright.

Drawing 3: Genesis 27:1–4—Isaac, sending Esau out for a hunt. Rebekah is eavesdropping.

Discuss **What is Isaac preparing to do?** (He is ready to give Esau the blessing, since he thinks he may die soon.) **Was Isaac supposed to give the blessing to Esau?** (Isaac certainly must have known that God told Rebekah that the blessing was to go to Jacob. Esau, too, must have known, but he willingly proceeded

Key Point
God worked through Jacob and Esau, despite their sin, to advance His plan of salvation. In spite of our sinful actions, God accomplishes His will and plan for our lives.

to do as his father had asked. Esau also knew that he had sold his birthright to Jacob and was not being honest to expect to receive the blessing.)

Drawing 4: Genesis 27:5–17—Rebekah with Jacob, who is dressed in his brother's clothes with animal skins on his neck and hands, holding the prepared food.

Discuss **Why would Rebekah tell Jacob what to do?** (Rebekah may continually remember God's words to her regarding Jacob's future. She knows the blessing is supposed to go to Jacob, and she is determined that it will. Rebekah's actions show a lack of faith in God's ability or willingness to keep His promise.) **Was Jacob right to obey his mother's directions?** (While it is right to honor one's parents, Jacob knew that what he was doing was wrong. He knew the plan would require lying to his father. By going along with her plan, he, too, shows a lack of faith that God will keep His promise.)

Drawing 5: Genesis 27:18–29—Isaac blessing Jacob.

Discuss **Jacob lies boldly to his father, and although Isaac is confused by the voice, he believes Jacob is Esau and gives the blessing. What commandment is broken here?** (Jacob breaks the Eighth Commandment, which forbids lying. Point out that Jacob also told Isaac that God had granted him success in his hunt. This is blasphemy—telling lies about God. We are all sometimes tempted to covet, lie, or deceive, especially to achieve something for ourselves. But God forgives all our sins for Jesus' sake if we repent and ask for forgiveness.)

Drawing 6: Genesis 27:30–40—Esau, distraught, receiving his father's words.

Discuss **Isaac trembled violently when he realized he had given the blessing to Jacob. Esau cried when he found out there was no blessing left for him. Did they get what they deserved?** It was wrong for Rebekah and Jacob to trick them in order to get the blessing. But Isaac knew that by giving the blessing to Esau he would have been acting contrary to God's will. He realized he had been lied to, and this probably was very hurtful to him. We can see that God's will would be done, in spite of how humans try to manipulate a situation. Esau also knew that Jacob was to have the blessing and that he had sold his birthright. Esau may have hoped he'd receive it anyway, but the finality of the realization was devastating. The whole family broke the First Commandment. They are also guilty of a lack of faith in God's ability or willingness to keep His promise to them. Instead they manipulated one another for selfish gain. Use the Faith Word Card *trust* to conclude that a lack of faith results in a lack of trust. Isaac's words to Esau, instead of a blessing, were only a prediction of what was to become of Esau and his descendants.

Say **In spite of the sinful actions of Isaac, Rebekah, Jacob, and Esau, God's will was carried out. Jacob later became Israel, the father of the great nation, and Esau** [EE saw] (Edom [EE dum]) **became the leader of the Edomites. The Edomites would be a fighting people, but they would never be as strong as the Israelites, just as God had told Rebekah before they were born.**

3 We Live (15 minutes)

Direct the students to page 3 of the leaflet, "God's Good Work," and assign verses to students to read aloud: Ephesians 2:8–9; 1 Corinthians 1:7–9; Philippians 1:6, 11; Romans 10:17; and 1 Peter 3: 21. As a class, discuss the questions.

Lesson 10

- **Ephesians 2:8–9—What is the good work?** Faith in Christ and salvation
- **1 Corinthians 1:7–9—What is the day of Christ Jesus?** The end of the age, our own death, or the second coming of Jesus
- **Philippians 1:6, 11—Who began the good work?** God the Father
- **Romans 10:17; 1 Peter 3:21—By what means does God begin this good work?** Through the preaching of the Word and Baptism

Ask Does Philippians 1:6 refer to any good works we have done or may do in the future? (No, it is a gift from God [Ephesians 2:8–9].)

Say As we read our Bible text for today's study, think about these questions and how they relate to the people in the Bible account. Especially note that God had a plan for Jacob. It was God who carried it on to completion in spite of Jacob's sin of coveting and his sinful actions. Even though we are sinful, God works in us to accomplish His will. God forgives all of our sins for Jesus' sake. Jesus died on the cross and rose again so that we are forgiven. Turn to page 4 of the Lesson Leaflet, and read together the Bible Words. Remind students of the definitions of *trust* and *faith*.

Play and sing the Bible Words song from the CD, track 14. Make copies of Bible Words Puzzle 10 for students to complete now or at home.

Ask How does trust enable us to believe this Bible verse? Who is it that "began the good work" in us, and when is the day of Christ Jesus? (Trust is what helps us to be confident that God will do as He has promised. God has a plan for each of us, and it is comforting to know that even if we sin and disobey God, we won't somehow disrupt His plan. God does all things in His own time. God is always at work in us and will perfect us through Jesus Christ. Our best prayer is one that asks for God's will to be done.)

Say This doesn't give us permission to do whatever we want and God will make it right. It is assurance that when we sin, we will not keep God from accomplishing His work. Through Jesus, God forgives our sins. God comes to us in His Sacraments of Baptism and Holy Communion. God comes to us with forgiveness of sins.

4 Closing (5 minutes)

When the students have uncovered the brief prayer ("Thy will be done"), have a volunteer read the paragraph below it. Review the Third Petition and its explanation (Small Catechism or Resource Page 3).

Say It is important for us to remember that the devil wants us to think we can do things for ourselves, without waiting for God or asking for His guidance. We sin when we want to do it all ourselves without God. Our Bible Words for today remind us that even when our sinful nature makes us impatient like Jacob, God will forgive us and continue to work in our lives. God's will for us is for our own good and in God's own time.

Sing the hymn, "If God Himself Be for Me" (*LSB* 724; CD 4). Distribute copies of Reproducible Page 10 for a take-home activity. Suggest that they may want to make and share this soup with a busy family.

Close with the Lord's Prayer.

Key Point
God worked through Jacob and Esau, despite their sin, to advance His plan of salvation. In spite of our sinful actions, God accomplishes His will and plan for our lives.

Liturgy Link
Numbers 6:22–27 is the Aaronic Blessing spoken by the pastor at the end of the Divine Service. God spoke this blessing to Moses, who gave it to Aaron to speak to God's people. God blesses us in His Divine Service each Sunday morning.

Ask an adult to help you. Rinse and drain lentils. Put all ingredients into a saucepan. Heat to boiling; then, reduce the heat. Cover and cook gently about 30 minutes until lentils and carrots are tender. Makes 2 servings.

Esau sold his birthright to Jacob for a bowl of lentils. Even though lentils are a tasty food, God's will and blessing should have been more important to Esau than lunch! When we pray the Third Petition of the Lord's Prayer, we ask God to provide what is best for us, even if it's not what we think we want. Thank God for the many blessings He provides, such as your food, clothes, and home. Ask Him for faith that keeps His will as your most important blessing.

Third Petition of the Lord's Prayer

Thy will be done on earth as it is in heaven.

What does this mean? The good and gracious will of God is done even without our prayer, but we pray in this petition that it may be done among us also.

How is God's will done? God's will is done when He breaks and hinders every evil plan and purpose of the devil, the world, and our sinful nature, which do not want us to hallow God's name or let His kingdom come;

and when He strengthens and keeps us firm in His Word and faith until we die.

This is His good and gracious will.

UPPER ELEMENTARY

Preparing the Lesson

Jacob's Dream

Genesis 27:41–28:22

Lesson 11

_____
Date of Use

Key Point

God revealed the certainty of His presence now and forever to Jacob in a dream. God reveals Himself and His plan of salvation for us in His Word and Sacraments. We respond with praise and worship.

Law/**Gospel**

I sin when I think God does not care for me or has left me alone. **God promises in His Word never to leave me. His gracious love for me, revealed through His Son, Jesus, moves my heart to worship and praise Him.**

Context

This account shows the consequences of Rebekah and Jacob's deception of Isaac. It also shows how the Lord upholds His children even as they experience the consequences of sin and how He works in their lives and circumstances to accomplish His purposes.

Commentary

Esau hates Jacob because of the blessing Isaac gave to Jacob, a blessing Esau thinks should have gone to him. When Rebekah hears that Esau plans to kill Jacob, she urges Jacob to go to Laban, her brother, until Esau's anger cools. Rather than tell Isaac about Esau's plot, she instead relates how unhappy she will be if Jacob marries one of the pagan women of the land. Then Isaac directs Jacob to go to Laban and take as a wife one of Laban's daughters. Before sending him on his way, Isaac blesses Jacob with the blessing given to Abraham.

Jacob faces a long, dangerous journey and a painful separation from his parents. Jacob is forced to leave the land that God promised to his grandfather, his father, and now to him. He must take it on faith that God will one day bring him back. But as painful and uncertain as the situation is, God is working in it to provide Jacob with a wife through whom Jacob's greatest descendant, Jesus, would be born.

One night during Jacob's journey, God appears to him in a dream. In the dream, Jacob sees a ladder (or possibly a stairway) set up on earth, with its top in heaven. Angels ascend and descend on the ladder. This dream assures Jacob that God's angels travel from earth to heaven, relaying Jacob's needs to God, and from heaven back to earth to meet those needs.

At the top of the ladder, the Lord Himself appears and reaffirms to Jacob the promises first made to Abraham: that God will give the land of Canaan to Jacob and his offspring, who will be as numerous as dust on the earth, and that through Jacob's offspring all the families on the earth will be blessed. Furthermore, God promises to watch over Jacob and bring him back to this land.

When Jacob awakes, he is awestruck. He marks the place with a pillar, consecrates it, and calls it Bethel, which means "house of God." Then in thanksgiving, he makes a vow to God. Although the vow reveals Jacob's continuing uncertainty about the future, in it he entrusts himself to God's care.

Jesus alludes to Jacob's dream when He says, "Truly, truly, I say to you, you will see heaven opened, and the angels of God ascending and descending on the Son of Man" (John 1:51). As the ladder in Jacob's dream was a bridge between heaven and earth, so Jesus is the ultimate bridge between God and mankind. He is both true God and true man. By His suffering, death, and resurrection, Jesus reconciled sinful humanity to God, and He is the source of eternal blessings for all who trust in Him.

To hear an in-depth discussion of this Bible account, visit cph.org/podcast and listen to our Seeds of Faith podcast each week.

Lesson 11

Jacob's Dream
Genesis 27:41–28:22

Connections

Bible Words
How awesome is this place! This is none other than the house of God, and this is the gate of heaven. Genesis 28:17

Faith Word
eschatology, Bethel, Alpha and Omega, patriarch

Hymn
How Firm a Foundation (*LSB* 728; CD 3)

Catechism
Apostles' Creed: First and Third Articles
Lord's Prayer: Second Petition
Luther's Morning Prayer (CD 21)

1 Opening (10 minutes)

Have available crayons and copies of Reproducible Page 11, "The End," found at the end of this lesson. As the students arrive, have them each draw a picture depicting an ending. It could be a storybook "happily ever after," an athletic victory in "double overtime," a move to another state, a funeral, or any other ending. When all of the students have gathered, celebrate Baptism anniversaries and birthdays and gather offerings. Make the sign of the cross, and lead the students in the Invocation.

Say In the name of the Father and of the Son and of the Holy Spirit. Amen.

Pray Dear heavenly Father, thank You for bringing us to church. It is Your house, the gate of heaven. We thank You that You are always with us and that we see You in Your Word and Sacraments. Send Your Holy Spirit to be with us this day and through all our endings and our beginnings. We pray this in Jesus' name. Amen.

Sing "How Firm a Foundation" (*LSB* 728; CD 3).

Ask the students to share their "ending" drawings. Point out that every ending also allows for a new beginning: stories have sequels, sports seasons recycle, moving brings new experiences and friends, funerals mark the beginning of a believer's eternal life. Allow a moment for them to decide the corresponding "beginning" for their "end" picture and to write it on the line.

MATERIALS NEEDED

1 Opening	2 God Speaks	3 We Live	4 Closing
Teacher Tools	**Teacher Tools**	**Teacher Tools**	**Teacher Tools**
Faith Word Cards 41, 43	Faith Word Cards 42, 44	Poster C	CD
CD	Posters A and B	CD	Faith Word Cards 1–44
Other Supplies	**Student Stuff**	**Student Stuff**	**Other Supplies**
Reproducible Page 11 (TG)	Bible Discovery Guide (optional)	Lesson Leaflets	Resource Page 6 (TG; optional)
	Lesson Leaflets	**Other Supplies**	Mobile device (optional)
		Resource Page 3 (TG)	
		Luther's Small Catechism (optional)	

84

Say Endings and beginnings are exciting—finishing a big project, moving to a new city, joining a new team. Today, we will study an ending and a beginning for Jacob, Isaac's youngest son. He is leaving one life behind and starting over in a new place. The Church recognizes that there will be an ending to this earthly life for all of us, when Jesus will come for a second time, gathering all believers to Himself in heaven. We call those days the *end times*. We have a big word that means the "study of the end times." Show this definition on the Faith Word Card *eschatology*. Then, reveal the word. Let students try to pronounce it. **It is called eschatology** (ess kuh TOL uh jee).

Show the Faith Word Card *Alpha and Omega*. Discuss that earth as we know it had a beginning and will have an end, but that God has always been God, without beginning or end. He is our "firm foundation." Encourage them to share the Faith Words on Reproducible Page 11 or the Lesson Leaflet with their families.

2 God Speaks (20 minutes)

Say **Our Bible study about Jacob's ending and beginning includes the familiar passage about Jacob's dream.** Show Poster B, pointing out Canaan, Paddan Aram, Haran, and Bethel. Quickly refer to Poster A to show the time the events of today's story occurred. Also review "God's Family Tree" on Poster B or page 3 of the Bible Discovery Guide. Have the students turn to Genesis 27:41–28:22. Ask the students to take turns reading one verse at a time. Let students pass if they prefer.

Discuss **When our story begins, Esau is very angry because Jacob has tricked him out of his blessing. Esau wants to kill Jacob. How does this affect the whole family?** (The whole family suffers consequences because of their sinful actions. Jacob fears for his life. Perhaps Rebekah fears that Esau might be killed in revenge if he kills Jacob. Isaac realizes that he cannot change God's plan, and his words of blessing to Esau show that now they must accept God's plan. Rebekah must send her favorite son away for what will be twenty years. In spite of the family's sinful actions, God will work all for good. Rebekah is still not completely honest with Isaac.)

Why does she say she wants Jacob sent away? How does Esau also respond to this? (Rebekah says she doesn't want Jacob to marry a Canaanite. She wants Jacob to marry one of her brother's daughters.) **To please his parents, Esau, who had married a Canaanite woman, marries again, this time to a daughter of Ishmael. However, the Ishmaelites—descendants of Abraham's son by Hagar—were outside of God's promise and probably no more pleasing to them than the Canaanites.**

Describe Jacob's dream. What is important about the angels going up and down the stairs to God? (The angels traveling up the stairs show Jacob's requests being carried to God; the descending angels show God's love and care coming down to earth. God Himself stood at the top of the stairs and made His promise to Jacob. The promise that God makes to Jacob in his dream is the same promise that God made to Abraham.) **What exactly did God promise? Who are the descendants God is talking about?** (He promised that Jacob would possess the land he was lying on and that his descendants would be as numerous as the dust of the earth. All people would be

Key Point
God revealed the certainty of His presence now and forever to Jacob in his dream. God reveals Himself and His plan of salvation for us in His Word and Sacraments; we respond with praise and worship.

blessed through Jacob. God also promises to remain with Jacob. All believers will be blessed because of Jacob's most important descendant, Jesus. We are among the blessed families of earth. Just as God promised He would not leave Jacob, He has also promised to be with us always.) **How does Jacob respond when he wakes from his dream? How is this the same for us?** (He is frightened and amazed.)

Refer to the Bible Words on page 4 of the Lesson Leaflet. Show the Faith Word Card *Bethel*.

Say **Jacob set the stone he'd used under his head on end, anointed it with oil, and named the place *Bethel*, or "House of God." The vow that Jacob makes in verses 20–22 is not a conditional bargaining tool. He wasn't trying to make a deal with God. Rather, it is a statement that because God has promised to care for him and to remain with him, Jacob's response could be nothing other than worship and praise. Our response, too, is worship and praise. Without our Savior, Jesus, we would be lost. He died and rose from the dead so we could be forgiven. By faith in Him, we have eternal life.**

Endings and Beginnings

Complete the activities on page 2 of the Lesson Leaflet. Before beginning the first activity, you may need to explain the Faith Word *patriarch*. Hold up the Faith Word Card. Invite students to say the word and to suggest a meaning for the word. When all have shared their ideas, say the word for the students and let them read the definition.

Say **Abraham, Isaac, and now Jacob are considered the patriarchs of a great nation.**

The matched phrases are as follows:
Jacob had to leave home—God prepares Jacob to be patriarch of a great nation
High school graduation—First day of college
Jesus died and rose again—My sins are forgiven, and I will go to heaven
Omega—Alpha

A Letter From Bethel

Children may have difficulty imagining themselves as Jacob for *A Letter from Bethel*. Restate the directions as, "What would Jacob tell his parents?" Children with learning disabilities may have difficulty writing their own words for this activity. Allow them to use another student or an adult helper as a scribe.

Lesson 11

3 We Live (20 minutes)

Say Leaving his home was an ending for Jacob. He had to leave behind everything and everyone he knew in order to save his life. **How do you think Jacob felt?** (Fearful, uncertain, anxious) **Predict what new beginning will happen to Jacob, now that he has heard God's promise again.** (God promises to be with Jacob, and Jacob's coming experiences will strengthen his faith and prepare him to become the patriarch of a great nation.)

Talk about how we sin or face similar temptations to sin. Children at this age have many fears, real and imagined. Be sensitive to this. Give students time to think about these questions, and encourage discussion. Always remember to emphasize the Gospel.

Ask **When do we not trust God to take care of us? When do we think God has left us alone? Do we ever doubt that we are saved from sin and death?**

Has there ever been a time when you don't *feel* like your parents' child? Does that change the fact that you *are* your parents' child? Allow for discussion.

Say **When we don't feel like God is with us, or when we feel that God is not protecting or providing for us, the facts don't change—God loves us, promises to provide for us, and has made us His precious children through Holy Baptism. We have been sealed, or marked, with water and His Word. That is a fact—a sure and certain hope that does not change!**

Direct the students' attention to the Bible Words on page 4 of the Lesson Leaflet. Divide the verse into three parts at the punctuation marks, and assign each part to a group of students. Have each group stand and say their words in turn, first while looking at the leaflet and then without looking. If you have time, have the group change parts until all three sections of the verse are committed to memory. Then, continue with this explanation.

Say **Jacob named the place where he slept and dreamed of Jesus "Bethel." He called it the gate to heaven; he saw God there, and God promised that He would always be with Jacob. He promises to always be with us also. Where is God present with us today?** (God reveals Himself to us today in His Word and Sacraments. He is present with us every Sunday when we celebrate the Divine Service. The Words of Institution in the Divine Service tell us He is present in Holy Communion. We receive the Holy Spirit in Baptism. The explanation of the First Article of the Apostles' Creed also assures us that He is with us.)

Distribute copies of "How Firm a Foundation" (*LSB* 728; CD 3); melody-line scores or lyrics can be printed from the teacher CD. Remind the students of the assurances of God's promise to be with us in this hymn, especially stanzas 2 through 5, which are written as though God Himself were speaking. Sing the hymn together.

Continue **Jacob had taken matters into his own hands to make things go his way. In spite of that, God made everything work out the way He wanted. What prayers do we pray that ask God to do His will among us?** Allow responses. Remind the students of the Second and Third Petitions of the Lord's Prayer, "Thy kingdom come" and "Thy will be done" (point them out on Poster C). Read the explanation to the class found on Resource Page 3.

www.cph.org

Lesson 11

Key Point

God revealed the certainty of His presence now and forever to Jacob in his dream. God reveals Himself and His plan of salvation for us in His Word and Sacraments; we respond with praise and worship.

God Protects Me

Say Like Jacob, we respond with worship and praise. Turn to page 3 of the Lesson Leaflet and complete the activity "God Protects Me." Ask a student to read the introductory paragraph. You may wish to work through this activity together to provide the students with some of the references from Luther's Small Catechism. The texts are also included in the resource pages at the end of the Teacher Guide. Correct answers are italicized.

1. In Baptism, God gives us His *Holy Spirit*. John 3:5
2. Angels *guard* us. Psalm 91:11–12
3. *Angel* means "messenger."
4. God *defends* me against all danger. First Article
5. God guards and *protects* me from all evil. First Article
6. Let your holy angel be *with* me. Luther's Morning Prayer
7. . . . that the *evil foe* may have no power over me. Luther's Morning Prayer
8. On the Last Day, God will *raise* me and all the dead. Third Article Explanation
9. . . . and give *eternal life* to me and all believers in Christ. Third Article Explanation
10. Thy *kingdom* come. Second Petition

4 Closing (5 minutes)

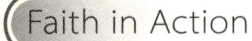

Say Let's review. Remind the students about studying the First Article, God the Creator and Preserver. Play and sing the songs from the CD. Ask volunteers to identify their favorite stories and hymns and to explain their choices. You could record this time on your mobile device and share the video with Sunday School parents. Consider playing the video in the hallway next week while parents wait to pick up their kids from Sunday School. Direct their attention to the Gospel message in each story—that God preserves His people and has promised to send His Son, the Savior.

Play Faith Words Baseball using all Faith Word Cards from Lessons 1 through 11 and the directions below (or on Resource Page 6).

Games—Faith Words Baseball

Use the basic rules of baseball with some variation. Designate the bases and home plate along four walls of the classroom area. The teacher stands/sits in the middle to pitch.

Divide the class into two teams. "Pitch" to the first team member by picking a card and reading the word to the student, allowing him or her to give the meaning. If it is correct, the "batter" advances to the first base position. If the player misses the definition, that team gets an out. Continue play in this fashion until the team gets three outs, and play moves to the other team.

A variation of the singles-only game is to decide before the game which words are more difficult. Mark the more difficult terms as doubles, triples, or home runs. When the player comes up "to bat," ask which type of question he or she wants:

Lesson 11

a single, double, etc. *Option:* Add special cards that say, "home run," "grand slam," "double-play (two outs)," and so forth. If one of the special cards is drawn, that team automatically gets whatever the card reads.

After the game, conclude with a song and prayer. Make copies of Bible Words Puzzle 11 for students to take home.

Sing again "How Firm a Foundation" (*LSB* 728; CD 3).

Pray Dear heavenly Father, You are the Alpha and the Omega, the beginning and the end. We thank You that You have promised to be with Your children and that You remain with us today. Forgive us when we fail to trust You and when we feel we are alone. Because of Your Son, Jesus, we look forward to our new beginning in heaven. In Jesus' name we pray. Amen.

Teacher Tip

If you have students with learning disabilities who struggle to remember the definitions to the faith words or Bible memory work, let them "pitch" (with help, if necessary) by selecting the card and/or reading the words to the batter.

The End

Draw a picture of an ending. It can be an ending that you have experienced, like moving away from your town or an end to an athletic event. Or it can be a story you know, a "happily ever after."

Endings bring new beginnings! What new beginning results from the ending you drew?

_____

As Christians, we remember that our days on earth are limited (an ending) and that we will spend eternity in heaven (a beginning!). Here are some "ending and beginning" words.

eschatology (ess kuh TOL uh jee): Study of the end times, the last days of earth as we know it

Alpha (AL fuh): Greek for "beginning"

Omega (oh MEG uh): Greek for "ending"

heaven (HEV un): The home of believers for all eternity

"I am the Alpha and the Omega," says the Lord God, "who is and who was and who is to come, the Almighty." Revelation 1:8

"It is done! I am the Alpha and the Omega, the beginning and the end. To the thirsty I will give from the spring of the water of life without payment. The one who conquers will have this heritage, and I will be his God and he will be My son." Revelation 21:6–7

UPPER ELEMENTARY

Preparing the Lesson

Jacob's Family

Genesis 29:1–30:24

Lesson 12

_____
Date of Use

Key Point

Through Jacob's family, God brought forth the Savior, Jesus Christ, who endured lies, deception, and the schemes of sinful mankind to work our salvation on the cross.

Law/**Gospel**

I sin when I lie or deceive others. **In spite of my sin, God blesses me with my family and all that I need and forgives me for the sake of His own Son, Jesus.**

Context

Jacob, with the aid of his mother, Rebekah, had deceived his twin brother, Esau, and his father, Isaac. Because Esau was so angry with him, Rebekah, afraid for Jacob's life, convinced Isaac to send him to his uncle Laban (Rebekah's brother) to find a wife. On the journey, God came to Jacob in a dream, renewing the threefold promise that He had previously made with Abraham (Genesis 12:3; 28:14).

Commentary

The deceiver was deceived. After Jacob deceived his father and brother, his uncle Laban deceived him in marriage. Jacob did not get the bride of his choosing until he promised to work for another seven years.

Jacob loves Rachel more than Leah. This causes competition within the marriage. Jacob fulfills his marital duty with Leah only out of obligation. Despite this jealousy, God intercedes and works His will. Leah becomes the mother of Jacob's sons. One of her sons will be the father of God's line of priests; another will be the father of King David and ultimately of Jesus Christ. Leah is blessed. God looks upon the oppressed and distraught and gives blessings without measure. Leah's dishonor as the "unloved" wife is overshadowed and vanquished by the lineage of the Messiah.

It is now Rachel's turn to feel dishonored. Barrenness is a heavy cross for a woman to bear. Barrenness excludes Rachel from participating in creation's ordinance of being fruitful and multiplying. It also excludes her from God's promise to Eve that a woman would bear the Seed that will crush the serpent's head. Her husband loves her, but she is not able to produce the fruit of that love. By God's grace, however, Rachel receives an answer to her prayer and gives birth to Joseph and Benjamin, Jacob's favorite sons.

Laban's sinful deception, Jacob's sinful favoritism, and the sisters' sinful jealousy and competition are unable to thwart God's promise. God works His good. The family of Abraham expands. The twelve tribes of Israel wait only for the birth of Benjamin. God's course of action is never derailed because of the sinfulness of His people. Nothing can stop His love. The world will be blessed through this family despite their past, present, and future sinfulness. Despite the insurmountable odds, God would become man through Abraham's family. Jesus would live, suffer, and die even for the sins of His ancestors.

To hear an in-depth discussion of this Bible account, visit cph.org/podcast and listen to our Seeds of Faith podcast each week.

Lesson 12
Jacob's Family
Genesis 29:1–30:24

Bible Words
For I know the plans I have for you, declares the LORD, plans for welfare and not for evil, to give you a future and a hope. Jeremiah 29:11 (CD 11)

Faith Words
kinsman, blessing, god, fear

Hymn
Praise God, from Whom All Blessings Flow (*LSB* 805; CD 5)

Catechism
First Commandment

Liturgy Link
Aaronic Blessing

Prepare to Teach

Make copies of Reproducible Page 12 on heavy cardstock paper.

Before the students arrive, display the Posters A, B, and C.

1 Opening (5 minutes)

Help your students develop a sense of awe and reverence for worship during the Opening. If you have your Opening in your classroom, set up an altar area, perhaps with liturgical paraments, candles, and a Bible. Let students volunteer to light candles, gather offerings, distribute hymnals, and do other tasks that will help them actively participate and feel a part of the worship experience.

Play the CD softly as the students arrive. Greet students as they arrive, especially any new students or visitors.

A Great Idea! → On the chalkboard, whiteboard, or a large piece of paper, make a simple family tree with your name at the bottom, your parents' names, and grandparents' names. Encourage students to make a family tree with their own family names following the pattern you have created. Show them the genealogy of Abraham's family on Poster B, "Father Abraham." Encourage casual conversation between students as they compare the family trees.

When all of the students have gathered, show students how to make the sign of the cross and explain that in this action, along with the words of the Invocation, which are also spoken at Baptism, they are reminded of their Baptism and of all the blessings they receive as God's children.

MATERIALS NEEDED

1 Opening	2 God Speaks	3 We Live	4 Closing
Teacher Tools	**Teacher Tools**	**Teacher Tools**	**Teacher Tools**
Posters A, B, and C	Faith Word Cards 45–48	Poster A	CD
CD	Posters A, B, and C	**Other Supplies**	
	CD	Reproducible Page 12 (TG)	
	Bible Review Cards 1–96		
	Student Stuff		
	Lesson Leaflets		
	Bible Discovery Guide		
	Other Supplies		
	Resource Page 7 (TG; optional)		

92

Lesson 12

Say In the name of the Father and of the Son and of the Holy Spirit. Amen.

Pray We thank You, Father, that You have brought us together today to hear Your Word and learn about Jacob and his family and how, in spite of human sin, You have blessed us with a Savior, Your Son, Jesus. In His name we pray. Amen.

2 God Speaks (20 minutes)

Jacob's Kinsmen

Show Faith Word Card *kinsman*, and discuss the meaning. Ask volunteers to show their family trees, identifying their kinsmen. Make casual observations about the relationship between children, parents, and grandparents. Use Faith Word Card *blessing* to help students understand that everything we have is a blessing from God.

Say We are blessed with families. Each family is unique and has its own special characteristics. Each family has at least one important fact in common—each is a gift from God. Today, we are going to learn about how God blessed Jacob with a family in spite of human sinfulness. We will also learn how and why Jacob's family is still important to us today.

Point out the time period of the story on Poster A. Provide background information from Growing in the Word or have students look briefly at Genesis 27–28 to find out why Jacob left home, where he was going, and how he had obtained the birthright from his brother, Esau, through trickery. Jacob was fleeing his brother's fury and had been sent to his mother's brother (Laban) in Haran to find a suitable wife.

Again use Faith Word Card *kinsman* to explain the relationship. Remind the students that it was on this same journey that Jacob had his dream of the stairway to heaven at Bethel (Genesis 28:10–22). At this time, God had promised to be with him and to give him many offspring. This promise was an extension of the promise God made to Jacob's grandfather Abraham. As today's story unfolds, we see that God is keeping His promise as Jacob finds his uncle's family and meets his future wives.

Today's Scripture reading is long and has many names. Distribute the Lesson Leaflets. Direct students to complete Part A of the activity on page 2 of the leaflet as you read the text aloud. (Be sure to practice pronouncing difficult names; pronunciations are found in the text below.) In the leaflet activity, the students will choose the appropriate name from the word bank and copy it into the column under the mother's name: Leah, Rachel, Zilpah (ZILL pah), or Bilhah (BILL hah). Pause your reading when you come to the birth of a son and direct the students to the correct responses. Note that the numbers in the columns show the birth order of the sons.

Key Point

Through Jacob's family, God brought forth the Savior, Jesus Christ, who endured lies, deception, and the schemes of sinful humankind to work our salvation on the cross.

Have the students match the names of other family members to the correct choice in Part B. You may also refer the students to Poster B or the genealogy on page 3 of the Bible Discovery Guide for help. Correct responses follow:

Leah's Sons	Rachel's Sons	Zilpah's Sons	Bilhah's Sons
1. Reuben (ROO ben)	11. Joseph	7. Gad	5. Dan
2. Simeon	12. Benjamin	8. Asher was born later.	6. Naphtali (NAF tuh lee)
3. Levi			
4. Judah			
9. Issachar (IHZ ah car)			
10. Zebulun (ZEBB you lun)			

Dinah is Leah's daughter (c); Rebekah is Jacob's mother (a); Isaac is Jacob's father (d); and Laban is Jacob's uncle (b).

Discuss What arrangement did Jacob make with Laban? (Jacob became a herdsman for his uncle. Laban allowed Jacob to name his wages, perhaps knowing already how much Jacob loved Rachel. The two men agreed that Jacob would work for seven years in order to have Rachel for his wife.) **How did Laban trick Jacob? How did they agree to correct the situation?** (After seven years, Laban agreed to give Rachel as Jacob's wife. However, Laban switched his daughters so that Jacob actually married Leah, Rachel's older sister. Laban would also give Rachel to Jacob, but Jacob would have to work another seven years.) **This trick by Laban was a sin. He did not keep his word to Jacob. He was being selfish, knowing that Jacob would continue to work for him for no other pay than having Rachel for his wife.**

In spite of human sinfulness and deceit, God still blessed Jacob, Leah, and all humankind. How? (Leah would bear Jacob the son through whose line the Savior would be born. Jacob and Leah's fourth son, Judah, would be an ancestor of King David and Jesus.)

Have students look at the genealogy of Jesus in Matthew 1 to find the name of Judah (v. 3), King David (v. 6), and Jesus (v. 16).

Say Through Jacob's family, God brings forth the Savior, Jesus Christ, who endured lies, deception, and the schemes of sinful humankind to work our salvation on the cross. Was Laban more deceitful than some people today? Why do you think so? Was the way Laban tricked Jacob any different from how people treat one another today? Allow for discussion. **In our own families and among our friends, we sometimes find ourselves in situations where there is deception. We sin when we lie and deceive or trick others. In spite of our sin, God blesses us with all that we need, including our families. Because of sin, we suffer from the lies and deceitful actions of our families, friends, and others.** Ask students to give examples. **Jesus suffered lies and deception for us on the cross to earn our salvation.**

Ask How did Jacob feel about his wives? (Jacob loved Rachel more than Leah.) **This led to competition between the sisters, and it ultimately led to their sinful actions of giving their servant girls to Jacob in order to have more children.** (You may want to explain to the students that the names the mothers chose for their sons reflect their thoughts and attitudes at the time of the birth. Judah, Leah's fourth son, is the first name given that praises God. Interestingly, it is through Judah's line that the Messiah will come.) **In spite of human sinfulness, God blessed Jacob with many children, just as He promised. God would send**

His Son, the Messiah, through this family. God's Son, the Savior, took all of the sins of Jacob and his family to the cross and graciously forgave them.

Point to Poster C, focusing on the Ten Commandments.

Ask What is sin? (Acts against God's Commandments; every thought, desire, word, or deed that is contrary to God's Law) **How do we know what sin is?** (God gives His Commandments to show us our sin, to help us to know what is right, and to help us live as Christians. They also show us our need for a Savior.)

Explain Even though God did not give the Ten Commandments until later in the history of His people, we can still use them to identify the sins of Jacob, Laban, and other figures in Bible stories.

Ask students to read the First Commandment and explanation from page 2 of the Lesson Leaflet.

Show Faith Word Cards *god* and *fear* and discuss the meanings.

Ask What kinds of things can become our gods? Encourage contemporary examples, such as money, video games, material possessions, or work. **When we seek other gods, we demonstrate a lack of trust in God's promises to love and care for us by attempting to provide for ourselves. What kinds of things could have become Jacob's gods?** (His children; his wives, especially Rachel, toward whom he showed much favoritism; his work) Accept all reasonable answers. **Jacob demonstrated a lack of trust in God when he agreed to take his wives' servant girls in order to have more children.**

Explain The First Commandment demands that we keep our focus on God Himself. He has promised to bless us and care for us. We sin when we do not trust God and His good plans for us. Through His Son, God accomplishes His gracious and loving plans for our lives. We can trust His Word, because His Word is truth. But even when we sin, we can know God forgives us for His Son's sake, and God continues to love and care for us.

God's Gifts of Love

Lead the students through the "God's Gifts of Love" activity on page 3 of the Lesson Leaflet, helping them to recognize that every item listed should be circled. Help the students understand that no matter how much they have or lack or how difficult it is to find joy in their daily lives, God loves all people and wants them to know Him and trust in Him. God doesn't promise that our lives will be easy; He promises that He will be with us and care for us throughout our lives. He has sent His Son, Jesus Christ, as the Savior of all people. Because He loves all people, He also provides all material blessings and needs for this life on earth. Unbelievers may feel that they have earned these blessings by their own merit, but God's children recognize all things as gifts from God, their heavenly Father. In joy and thankfulness, we can share gifts of love with others. Have students brainstorm ways they can show love to others around them this week.

Have the students turn to page 4 of the Lesson Leaflet and read aloud with you the Bible Words for today, Jeremiah 29:11. Then play and sing the Bible Words song once or twice (CD 11). With these words in mind, assist the children in writing, in their own words, a prayer of thanks on the lines provided on page 3 or write the words they suggest on the board or large paper.

Use the Bible Review Cards as a quick review of story facts. You may wish to play a Bible review game, such as Hot Potato Bible Review at the end of this guide (Resource Page 7).

Key Point

Through Jacob's family, God brought forth the Savior, Jesus Christ, who endured lies, deception, and the schemes of sinful humankind to work our salvation on the cross.

A Great Idea!

Lesson 12

3 We Live (20 minutes)

Genesis Review

Direct students to the table of contents in their Bibles. Ask them to summarize what they see. Answers could include observations about the divisions into Old and New Testaments; many books are names of people; the books are not alphabetical; and the like.

Say **The Bible is made up of many books. For the past few months, we have been focusing on the very first book, Genesis.**

You may want to direct the students' attention to Poster A, the Timeline. Invite students to look back over the lessons studied throughout this quarter. Emphasize how much history Genesis covers: from the beginning of time, through their lesson today, and even to the death of Joseph, one of the sons we learned about today.

Say **The Bible is the inspired Word of God. That means that God the Holy Spirit specifically told the authors what to write so His Word would be preserved for people for as long as they live on earth. When we study the Book of Genesis, we know that we are learning about the very first generations of people and God's story of salvation throughout all time.**

Distribute copies of Reproducible Page 12, "Genesis: In the Beginning," found at the end of this lesson. Invite students to complete the chart, reviewing all that they have learned over the past few months. When students reach the end of the chart, tell them that they will learn about this lesson next week. Encourage students to look forward to the lesson, anticipating new learning.

Conclude **Using our Timeline Poster and what you've learned the past several weeks, write summaries of each lesson. You can tuck this into your Bible in the Book of Genesis so that you can refer to it and review many highlights of this first book of the Bible.**

Teacher Tip
For a quick reference of all the lessons for this quarter to help students with Reproducible 12, turn to the Table of Contents at the beginning of this Teacher Guide.

4 Closing (5 minutes)

You may wish to encourage students to take their reproducible page home and store it in their personal Bible.

Play and sing again today's Bible Words, Jeremiah 29:11 (CD 11). Make copies of Bible Words Puzzle 12 for students to complete now or at home.

Say **These are words of God's promise to His people, who had been captives in Babylon for seventy years and whom He would restore to their own land of Israel. There is another promise of God to us too. We can count on God to care for us and to provide for our needs, just as He cared for Jacob. God gives us forgiveness and love in His comforting Holy Word. The burden of our sin is taken from us in the washing of our Baptism and in His body and blood in the Lord's Supper. Let's join in a special hymn of praise to our triune God, who cares for us.**

Direct their attention to "Praise God, From Whom All Blessings Flow" (*LSB* 805; CD 5). Explain that a doxology is a hymn or a stanza of a hymn that praises Father, Son, and Holy Spirit. Because we traditionally stand in respect to God when we sing a doxology, encourage your students to stand as you sing the doxology together.

Pray Dear God, You have blessed us with families and all that we have. You have given us Your Word and promised to be with us. For this we thank and praise You. Forgive us when we don't trust in You. Forgive us for the times when we have hurt family members by our words or actions. Continue to be with us this day and forevermore. In Jesus' name we pray. Amen.

Key Point

Through Jacob's family, God brought forth the Savior, Jesus Christ, who endured lies, deception, and the schemes of sinful humankind to work our salvation on the cross.

Genesis: In the Beginning

Over the past several weeks, you have studied a large portion of the first book of the Bible, Genesis. It has included a history of many different people and has shown God's love to His people from the very beginning. Fill out the information below to summarize what you have learned.

Bible Reading	Bible Account	Account Summary
Genesis 1:1–2:3	God Creates the World	
Genesis 1:26–2:25		
Genesis 3		
Genesis 4:1–16		
Genesis 6:1–9:17		God preserves all species of animals and Noah's family, but destroys the rest of sinful creation. He makes a promise to never flood the world again.
Genesis 12:1–9; 15:1–6; 17		
Genesis 18:1–15; 21:1–7		
Genesis 21:1–7; 22:1–19		
Genesis 24	Abraham's Visitors from Heaven	
Genesis 25:19–34; 27:1–40		
Genesis 27:41–28:22		
Genesis 29:1–30:24		
Genesis 31:1; 32–33	Esau Forgives Jacob	

UPPER ELEMENTARY

Preparing the Lesson
Esau Forgives Jacob
Genesis 31:3; 32–33

Lesson 13

_____
Date of Use

Key Point

Though Jacob was sinful and deceived his brother, God preserved his life and reconciled him with his brother, Esau. Through His Son, God preserves our lives. Jesus overcame sin and death on the cross to win our forgiveness, life, and salvation.

Law/**Gospel**

Broken families and failed friendships are the result of sin. **Jesus' forgiveness restores my broken relationship with God and can heal my broken earthly relationships as well.**

Context

God blessed Jacob with a large family and many earthly possessions while he lived and worked with Laban. At God's command, Jacob leaves his father-in-law and starts for the land of his fathers—the land of promise. Fearing Laban's wrath, Jacob flees with all that God has given him.

Because Jacob left in secret and Rachel stole her father's idols, Laban pursues Jacob. When Laban overtakes Jacob's group, the two discuss Jacob's departure and search in vain for the stolen idols. Jacob decries the unfair manner of Laban's treatment of him. They make a covenant together, and Jacob departs for the Promised Land with Laban's blessing.

Commentary

When Esau hears that Jacob is coming back, he gathers a group of four hundred men to meet Jacob. In his distress, Jacob prays for the Lord's intervention and help (Genesis 32:9–12). Jacob respeaks God's words into His ears. He reminds God of the promise of land and innumerable descendants He gave to his grandfather Abraham, to his father, Isaac, and to him.

God hears Jacob's prayer for deliverance and comes to wrestle with Jacob. Jacob limps away from this encounter, but not without first receiving a new name and a divine blessing. Jacob grappled with man in the womb (25:22, 26) for the family birthright. Now he struggles with God for a heavenly birthright. Israel ("God's fighter") is the name given to Jacob. It will become the coat of arms for the tribes of his twelve sons, who will be heirs of a heavenly birthright, struggling with both men and God.

The crown of Israel is the struggle between God and man in the person of the God-man, Jesus Christ. In Jesus, God struggles with men. Even more, He struggles for men. God's cosmic struggle for mankind does not end with a sore hip, but rather with a bruised heel (3:15).

The name of God is not yet revealed to Jacob. However, Jacob knows that God struggled with him, for God says, "You have striven with God and with men" (32:28). Jacob renames the place of this encounter Peniel ("the face of God"). Now, Esau meets Jacob not for war, but for peace.

To hear an in-depth discussion of this Bible account, visit cph.org/podcast and listen to our Seeds of Faith podcast each week.

Lesson 13
Esau Forgives Jacob
Genesis 31:3; 32–33

Connections

Bible Words
For I am sure that neither death nor life, nor angels nor rulers, nor things present nor things to come, nor powers, nor height nor depth, nor anything else in all creation, will be able to separate us from the love of God in Christ Jesus our Lord. Romans 8:38–39

Faith Word
forgive, reconcile, murder, wrestle

Hymn
If God Himself Be for Me (*LSB* 724; CD 4)

Catechism
Fifth Commandment

Prepare to Teach

Preparation for today's lesson is essential. The text covers three chapters in Genesis, which you will paraphrase. Be sure to read the text (including all of chapter 31 for background information) more than once, if possible, so you may fluently retell the story of Jacob's departure from his father-in-law, Laban, and his reunion with Esau. An outline has been provided to assist you. Before the students arrive, display Posters A and B, and arrange the Faith Word Cards *god, fear, blessing, kinsman* from Lesson 12 and *murder, reconcile, forgive, wrestle* from Lesson 13 on a tabletop. Make several copies of Reproducible Page 13C, found at the end of this lesson. Cut the individual strips apart and scatter them on the tabletop.

1 Opening (5 minutes)

Play the CD catechism songs softly as students gather.

As students arrive, ask them to work together to sort the examples given on the strips from the Reproducible Page 13C under the Faith Word Card that they best describe. The examples may describe more than one Faith Word Card. Invite students to write other examples on the blank strips, or you may write specific examples appropriate for your class. Sort these as well.

Take attendance, gather offerings, and celebrate birthdays and Baptism anniversaries. Begin with the Invocation when all of the students have gathered. Invite students to make the sign of the cross to remind them of their Baptism.

Say In the name of the Father and of the Son and of the Holy Spirit. Amen.

MATERIALS NEEDED

1 Opening	2 God Speaks	3 We Live	4 Closing
Teacher Tools	**Teacher Tools**	**Teacher Tools**	**Teacher Tools**
Posters A and B	Faith Word Cards 45–52	Poster A	CD
Faith Word Cards 49–52 (TG; Reproducible Pages 13A, 13B)	Posters A, B, and C	Bible Review Cards 89–104	**Student Stuff**
CD	CD	**Student Stuff**	Lesson Leaflets
Other Supplies	Bible Review Cards 97–104	Bible Discovery Guide	
Reproducible Page 13C (TG)	**Student Stuff**	Lesson Leaflets	
	Lesson Leaflets		
	Other Supplies		
	Resource Page 1 (TG; optional)		

Pray Dear heavenly Father, thank You for our families. Remind us that You have included us in Your family through Baptism. As we learn today of how Jacob saw You and struggled with You, send Your Spirit that we, too, may see how Your Son struggled for us on the cross and know that You are present with us in Your Word and Sacraments. In Jesus' name we pray. Amen.

2 God Speaks (25 minutes)

Draw the students' attention to the chart you have all created using the Faith Word Cards and Reproducible Page 13C strips. Discuss how the examples clarify the meaning of the words, reviewing the meanings as necessary. Especially point out that God forgives all of our sins through Jesus Christ.

Say All of these examples have to do with relationships. Broken families and failed friendships are a result of sin. Jesus' suffering and death restores our broken relationship with God and can heal our broken human relationships as well. We can be reconciled with each other. Sin separates us from God and from those we love. In Christ, nothing can separate us from the love of God. We are reconciled with God; He forgives us for Jesus' sake.

Have students find Romans 8:38–39 in their Bibles and invite volunteers to read the verses. Provide simple bookmarks so students can mark this place for easy reference later.

Then draw the students' attention to the Fifth Commandment on Poster C. Read Luther's explanation of the Fifth Commandment aloud. (You may want students to read it aloud together as it is printed on the poster or Resource Page 1.) Have students look up and read Matthew 5:22 and 1 John 3:15. Relate these two verses to the explanation of the commandment: even our angry, hurtful thoughts make us guilty of breaking this commandment.

Say Our story today is about Jacob. Jacob was in Haran because he had to flee from his brother, Esau. Jacob had gotten the birthright from Esau by tricking him. Esau was angry enough to kill Jacob. The relationship between Jacob and Esau was broken. Jacob went to his uncle Laban's home. There, Laban tricked and deceived Jacob, and the relationship between them was broken. But Jacob also married Leah and Rachel, and God blessed him with a large family, in spite of Laban's tricks and deceit. Today, our story shows us how God enabled these relationships to be restored.

Before written language, history was passed on orally. Today's story will be told in this oral tradition. If you like, invite your students to be seated on the floor with you as you tell the story, as perhaps families in Old Testament times were seated as stories were shared with kinsmen.

Before you begin, point out the appropriate time period on the timeline poster, Poster A, and have students find the regions of Canaan and Haran on the map on Poster B.

Have students find today's Bible Words, Romans 8:38–39, in their Bibles. Then give each student the Lesson Leaflet so they can also refer to the Bible Words on page 4. (Give students a few moments to examine the biblical art on the front

Key Point
Though Jacob was sinful and deceived his brother, God preserved his life and reconciled him with his brother, Esau. Through His Son, God preserves our lives. Jesus overcame sin and death on the cross to win our forgiveness, life, and salvation.

of the leaflet. Invite them to open their leaflet so they can enjoy looking at the picture but also so they can read the Bible Words as they listen to the story.) At appropriate places in the story (as suggested by the asterisks), have students read together or recite Psalm 91:10, "No evil shall be allowed to befall you, no plague come near your tent," as a reminder that God was with Jacob throughout these events, just as He is with us today.

Use the following outline to help you retell Genesis 31:3 and parts of the rest of that chapter but especially the text for today's lesson, Genesis 32–33.

I. After twenty years with Laban, the Lord told Jacob to go back to Canaan. (Genesis 31:3)
II. Although Jacob had worked hard for twenty years, Laban had been unfair and had changed Jacob's wages ten times. God had blessed Jacob in spite of this.
III. Without telling Laban, Jacob left as soon as possible with his four wives, children, and many cows, sheep, goats, camels, and donkeys. Rachel stole her father's household gods. (*Psalm 91:10)
IV. Laban was angry when he found out the family had run away. (Genesis 31:22–35)
   a. Laban hadn't been able to say goodbye; his household gods had been stolen.
   b. He took his kinsmen to follow them; God told Laban in a dream to be careful when dealing with Jacob.
V. Laban caught up with and confronted Jacob, saying he had the power to harm Jacob, but God had told him not to. Laban at least wanted his gods back.
VI. Jacob told Laban to search for his gods. Jacob, not knowing that Rachel had stolen them and was hiding them by sitting on them, told Laban that whoever had stolen them would die. (*Psalm 91:10)
VII. Jacob became angry with Laban. (Genesis 31:36–55)
VIII. They made a covenant: Jacob set up a stone as a pillar and the family made a heap of stones as a sign of a peaceful relationship. Jacob offered a sacrifice to God, and Laban went home. (*Psalm 91:10)
IX. Jacob continued on to meet his brother, Esau. (Genesis 32:1–23)
   a. Jacob saw angels and knew God was still with him.
   b. Jacob sent word to Esau that he was coming.
   c. Esau brought four hundred men to meet him, and Jacob was afraid.
X. Jacob divided his people into two groups.
   a. Jacob prayed a faithful prayer. (Genesis 32:9–12; read these verses aloud.)
   b. He chose animals to send ahead as gifts: 220 goats, 30 camels plus their young, 50 cattle, 30 donkeys.
   c. Jacob's servants traveled ahead, with one group of animals at a time.
   d. Jacob sent his family and possessions across the river, and he stayed alone one more night. (*Psalm 91:10)
XI. Jacob wrestled with God. (Genesis 32:24–32)
   a. A man wrestled with Jacob all night, touching Jacob's hip and dislocating it. Jacob hung on.

b. Jacob refused to release the man until Jacob received a blessing. The man revealed Himself to be the Lord and changed Jacob's name to Israel, thus showing how Jacob had grown in faith: the name *Jacob* means "heel-grabber," someone who takes advantage of others; the name *Israel* means "struggled with God and won." (*Psalm 91:10)

XII. Jacob met Esau. (Genesis 33:1–20)
 a. Jacob saw Esau and went to meet him, bowing seven times.
 b. Esau ran to meet Jacob. They embraced and cried with joy.

XIII. Jacob and Esau parted again, this time on loving terms.
 a Esau returned to his home in Edom, and Jacob moved to Canaan.

XIV. Jacob bought property, set up his tent, and built an altar there. (*Psalm 91:10)

Use the Bible Review Cards 97–104 to check for understanding of this lesson. Use any questions that you think are appropriate for the students in your class.

3 We Live (15 minutes)

Ask How did God enable the broken relationships in Jacob's family to be restored? Invite students to explain. (God prevented Laban from harming Jacob. Laban and Jacob made a covenant or agreement to not harm each other. God enabled Esau to forgive Jacob. Jesus' forgiveness restores broken relationships.) Refer to the picture on the front of the leaflet. Ask students to identify Jacob and Esau and note the facial expressions of the brothers and other family members.

Conclude No matter what our situation, God is with us, just as God was with Jacob. Jacob wrestled with God, both physically and spiritually, in today's story and throughout his lifetime. Even though God had promised Jacob the birthright, Jacob still tricked Isaac, his father, into giving it to him rather than Esau, his twin brother. Jacob had to move away from his family, afraid for his life. But God affirmed His promise to send the Savior through Jacob's family. This Savior would reconcile all of us to God, paying the full price for our sins.

Ask How did the Savior pay the price? (Jesus, the Savior of the world, died on the cross.)

Say Jacob struggled for his birthright with man and God. On the cross, Jesus struggled for our heavenly birthright, winning over sin and death. We are His redeemed and restored children.

Have the students repeat the Bible Words one more time, this time from memory. No matter what our worries, our salvation is secure, because God sent His Son to rescue us from our sins. He restored our relationship with God.

Bible Study Skills

Remind the students of how the Bible is divided: Old Testament (Books of Moses, History, Poetry, Major and Minor Prophets) and New Testament (Gospels/History, Epistles, Prophecy). Demonstrate again how a reference is read: name of the book, chapter, and verse separated by a colon. Remind students that the Bible references shown at the upper corners of the page spreads are like guide words in a dictionary.

Lesson 13

Key Point

Though Jacob was sinful and deceived his brother, God preserved his life and reconciled him with his brother, Esau. Through His Son, God preserves our lives. Jesus overcame sin and death on the cross to win our forgiveness, life, and salvation.

On the board or a large paper, write four or five references for the students to look up. (Try some well-known verses, such as John 1:29, Psalm 118:1, and Ephesians 2:8–9.) Guide the students in finding the references, identifying in which section the book belongs, whether it is Old Testament or New Testament, and so on.

Have students find page 4 in the Bible Discovery Guide. Discuss the layout of the Bible books, showing by the timeline that the books are grouped thematically, rather than chronologically. Compare the Bible Discovery Guide timeline with the timeline poster, Poster A. Point out that God inspired men to write the books of the Bible much later than the actual events occurred.

If time permits, review the past two lessons using Bible Review Cards for Lessons 12 and 13. While some students play the game, others may work through the activities in the Lesson Leaflet. "Jacob's Gifts to Esau" is a decoding activity. Correct answers are goats, sheep, camels, cattle, and donkeys. "Jacob's Journal" is a writing activity. "Reconciled!" is a number puzzle activity with this solution: "Esau ran to meet [Jacob] and embraced him."

4 Closing (5 minutes)

Have the students look at the text of the hymn "If God Himself Be for Me" (*LSB* 724; CD 4), using hymnals or lyric sheets (found on the CD). Read through the words together and relate them to daily life and to today's Bible Words—Romans 8:38–39. Sing the hymn, especially stanzas chosen by the students, if time permits. Make copies of Bible Words Puzzle 13 for students to complete now or at home.

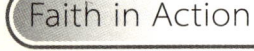

Encourage the students to practice their Bible study skills this week by looking up the Bible references (with their family members, if possible) found in the "Weekly Devotions" section on page 4 of the Lesson Leaflet. Families can work together to write down insights from the week's Bible readings. If you have a class email list, you can send a midweek reminder to families, encouraging them to share those insights with one another as well.

Pray Dear heavenly Father, we thank You that You keep Your promise to always be with us. Remind us as we go our separate ways that we are Your children through faith in Jesus Christ, Your dear Son and our Savior. In Jesus' name we pray. Amen.

forgive

Lesson 13   49

reconcile

Lesson 13   50

murder

Lesson 13   51

wrestle

Lesson 13   52

To excuse for a fault, offense, or sin; God, for Christ's sake, no longer holds our sins against us.

Lesson 13 49

To repair a broken relationship; to forgive each other and bring peace.

Lesson 13 50

To willfully cause the death of a human life out of hatred.

Lesson 13 51

To struggle physically or spiritually.

Lesson 13 52

Faith Word Card Review Activity

Angry words	Uncles, aunts, and cousins
Saying "I'm sorry"	Friendships
Physical struggle	God's gifts to His people
Spiritual struggle	Things that become more important to us than God's Word
Respect	Idols
Thinking angry thoughts about others	Knowing the right thing but not sure you'll do it
Helping someone who has hurt you	Being unsure of the right thing to do
Forgiving each other	Helping people in need
Holding a grudge	Saying "I forgive you"
Hurting someone on purpose	
Not holding a grudge	

THE COMMANDMENTS

The First Commandment

You shall have no other gods.

What does this mean? We should fear, love, and trust in God above all things.

The Fifth Commandment

You shall not murder.

What does this mean? We should fear and love God so that we do not hurt or harm our neighbor in his body, but help and support him in every physical need.

The Sixth Commandment

You shall not commit adultery.

What does this mean? We should fear and love God so that we lead a sexually pure and decent life in what we say and do, and husband and wife love and honor each other.

The Eighth Commandment

You shall not give false testimony against your neighbor.

What does this mean? We should fear and love God so that we do not tell lies about our neighbor, betray him, slander him, or hurt his reputation, but defend him, speak well of him, and explain everything in the kindest way.

The Ninth Commandment

You shall not covet your neighbor's house.

What does this mean? We should fear and love God so that we do not scheme to get our neighbor's inheritance or house, or get it in a way which only appears right, but help and be of service to him in keeping it.

THE APOSTLES' CREED

The First Article—CREATION

I believe in God, the Father Almighty, Maker of heaven and earth.

What does this mean? I believe that God has made me and all creatures; that He has given me my body and soul, eyes, ears, and all my members, my reason and all my senses, and still takes care of them. He also gives me clothing and shoes, food and drink, house and home, wife and children, land, animals, and all I have. He richly and daily provides me with all that I need to support this body and life. He defends me against all danger and guards and protects me from all evil. All this He does only out of fatherly, divine goodness and mercy, without any merit or worthiness in me. For all this it is my duty to thank and praise, serve and obey Him.

This is most certainly true.

The Second Article—REDEMPTION

And in Jesus Christ, His only Son, our Lord, who was conceived by the Holy Spirit, born of the Virgin Mary, suffered under Pontius Pilate, was crucified, died and was buried. He descended into hell. The third day He rose again from the dead. He ascended into heaven and sits at the right hand of God, the Father Almighty. From thence He will come to judge the living and the dead.

What does this mean? I believe that Jesus Christ, true God, begotten of the Father from eternity, and also true man, born of the Virgin Mary, is my Lord, who has redeemed me, a lost and condemned person, purchased and won me from all sins, from death, and from the power of the devil; not with gold or silver, but with His holy, precious blood and with His innocent suffering and death, that I may be His own and live under Him in His kingdom and serve Him in everlasting righteousness, innocence, and blessedness, just as He is risen from the dead, lives and reigns to all eternity.

This is most certainly true.

The Third Article—SANCTIFICATION

I believe in the Holy Spirit, the holy Christian church, the communion of saints, the forgiveness of sins, the resurrection of the body, and the life everlasting. Amen.

What does this mean? I believe that I cannot by my own reason or strength believe in Jesus Christ, my Lord, or come to Him; but the Holy Spirit has called me by the Gospel, enlightened me with His gifts, sanctified and kept me in the true faith.

In the same way He calls, gathers, enlightens, and sanctifies the whole Christian church on earth, and keeps it with Jesus Christ in the one true faith.

In this Christian church He daily and richly forgives all my sins and the sins of all believers.

On the Last Day He will raise me and all the dead, and give eternal life to me and all believers in Christ.

This is most certainly true.

THE LORD'S PRAYER

The Second Petition

Thy kingdom come.

What does this mean? The kingdom of God certainly comes by itself without our prayer, but we pray in this petition that it may come to us also.

How does God's kingdom come? God's kingdom comes when our heavenly Father gives us His Holy Spirit, so that by His grace we believe His holy Word and lead godly lives here in time and there in eternity.

The Third Petition

Thy will be done on earth as it is in heaven.

What does this mean? The good and gracious will of God is done even without our prayer, but we pray in this petition that it may be done among us also.

How is God's will done? God's will is done

when He breaks and hinders every evil plan and purpose of the devil, the world, and our sinful nature, which do not want us to hallow God's name or let His kingdom come;

and when He strengthens and keeps us firm in His Word and faith until we die.

This is His good and gracious will.

The Fourth Petition

Give us this day our daily bread.

What does this mean? God certainly gives daily bread to everyone without our prayers, even to all evil people, but we pray in this petition that God would lead us to realize this and to receive our daily bread with thanksgiving.

What is meant by daily bread? Daily bread includes everything that has to do with the support and needs of the body, such as food, drink, clothing, shoes, house, home, land, animals, money, goods, a devout husband or wife, devout children, devout workers, devout and faithful rulers, good government, good weather, peace, health, self-control, good reputation, good friends, faithful neighbors, and the like.

THE SACRAMENT OF HOLY BAPTISM

FIRST

What is Baptism?

Baptism is not just plain water, but it is the water included in God's command and combined with God's word.

Which is that word of God?

Christ our Lord says in the last chapter of Matthew: "Therefore go and make disciples of all nations, baptizing them in the name of the Father and of the Son and of the Holy Spirit." [Matthew 28:19]

SECOND

What benefits does Baptism give?

It works forgiveness of sins, rescues from death and the devil, and gives eternal salvation to all who believe this, as the words and promises of God declare.

Which are these words and promises of God?

Christ our Lord says in the last chapter of Mark: "Whoever believes and is baptized will be saved, but whoever does not believe will be condemned." [Mark 16:16]

THIRD

How can water do such great things?

Certainly not just water, but the word of God in and with the water does these things, along with the faith which trusts this word of God in the water. For without God's word the water is plain water and no Baptism. But with the word of God it is a Baptism, that is, a life-giving water, rich in grace, and a washing of the new birth in the Holy Spirit, as St. Paul says in Titus, chapter three:

"He saved us through the washing of rebirth and renewal by the Holy Spirit, whom He poured out on us generously through Jesus Christ our Savior, so that, having been justified by His grace, we might become heirs having the hope of eternal life. This is a trustworthy saying." [Titus 3:5–8]

FOURTH

What does such baptizing with water indicate?

It indicates that the Old Adam in us should by daily contrition and repentance be drowned and die with all sins and evil desires, and that a new man should daily emerge and arise to live before God in righteousness and purity forever.

Where is this written?

St. Paul writes in Romans chapter six: "We were therefore buried with Him through baptism into death in order that, just as Christ was raised from the dead through the glory of the Father, we too may live a new life." [Romans 6:4]

LUTHER'S MORNING PRAYER

I thank You, my heavenly Father, through Jesus Christ, Your dear Son, that You have kept me this night from all harm and danger; and I pray that You would keep me this day also from sin and every evil, that all my doings and life may please You. For into Your hands I commend myself, my body and soul, and all things. Let Your holy angel be with me, that the evil foe may have no power over me. Amen.

Game Directions

Games provided in the Teacher Tools can be made available for play for children who arrive early. They can be played on the Sunday they are introduced and any following Sunday. Faith Words Baseball and Basketball can both be introduced about halfway through the quarter (after students have learned a number of Faith Words). If you are team teaching, you may wish to share the games with the other teacher(s).

Faith Words Baseball

Needed for Play
Faith Word Cards

To Play
By about Lesson 7 or so in the quarter, the students will have studied a number of Faith Words. From that point on, you can play a review game with all Faith Word Cards studied so far. Play using the basic rules of baseball with some variation. Designate the bases and home plate along four walls of the classroom area. The teacher stands or sits in the middle to pitch.

Divide the class into two teams. "Pitch" to the first team member by picking a card and reading the word to the student and allowing him or her to give the meaning. If it is correct, the "batter" advances to the first base position. If the player misses the definition, that team gets an out. Continue play in this fashion until the team gets three outs; play moves to the other team.

A variation of the singles-only game is to decide before the game which words are more difficult. Mark the more difficult terms as doubles, triples, or homeruns. When the player comes "up to bat," ask which type of question he or she wants: a single, double, and so forth. *Option:* Add special cards that say "homerun," "grand slam," "double-play (two outs)," and so forth. If one of the special cards is drawn, that team automatically gets whatever the card reads.

Teacher Tip
If you have students with learning disabilities who struggle to remember the definitions to the faith words or Bible memory work, let them "pitch" (with help, if necessary) by selecting the card, reading the words to the batter, or both.

Hot Potato Bible Review

Use the Bible Review Cards from several lessons. Use a potato or ball or some other safe object that students can pass around. When they receive the potato, they are asked a question from the Bible Review Cards. If they answer correctly, they can choose the next student to whom the potato will be given. If they are incorrect, the teacher takes the potato and chooses a new player.

Faith Words Finger Twister

To reinforce the Faith Words for any lesson, have students write each of the four Faith Words from the lesson in random places on a blank sheet of paper. Read ONLY the definitions of the words for this activity, encouraging students to decide which Faith Word matches which definition.

Say **I am going to read a definition, and I want you to place your right thumb on the correct word.**

Make sure students don't see the word you choose. Read the definition and have students place their thumbs on the correct word. Continue reading the other definitions, having students place their pinky, first finger, and so forth on different words. You could make it even more fun by having them put an ear on one word, an elbow on another, or a thumb on a third.

Option: Include words from previous weeks. Also, you could place words on smaller scraps of paper and have students scatter them around their desks or table area. Continue play in like manner.

Faith Words Basketball

Needed for Play

Faith Word Cards

Options for a basket and ball:

- purchased mini basketball hoop with a sponge-type basketball
- container for "basket" and wadded-up piece of paper for "ball"
- mug and small ball to use on a tabletop

Object of the Game

Correctly identify Faith Words to earn points and shoot for basket points.

Options for Play

Choose Faith Word Cards for the game from the current or past quarter.

1. Provide a definition and ask students to identify the Faith Word that matches the definition.

2. Give a sentence that has the Faith Word missing.

3. Provide a synonym (a word that means the same thing) of the Faith Word and have the students identify the correct Faith Word.

4. Provide an antonym (a word that means the opposite) and have students identify the correct Faith Word.

For each of these options, be sure to have the Faith Words available for the students to see. The Faith Word Cards could be taped to the wall, or the words could be written on the board.

To Play

By about the fifth lesson or so, students will have studied enough Faith Words so that from that point on, you can play this review game with all Faith Word Cards studied so far.

Faith Words Basketball can be played with as few as two players and in as little as five minutes.

Divide the class into two to four teams. Ask the first student on the first team the Faith Word question. See "Options for Play." If a student identifies the correct Faith Word, that student earns a point *and* a chance to double his or her score by trying to shoot a basket. A successful shot earns the second point. There is no penalty for a missed shot.

After each missed Faith Word attempt or any basket attempt, play passes to the next team. If the student does not identify the correct Faith Word, pass the question to the next player on the next team. If the Faith Word is correctly guessed, use a new Faith Word Card. If the Faith Word isn't named correctly, come back to it later in the game.

At the end of the game, the team with the most points wins.

Glossary

Alpha and Omega The first and last letters of the Greek alphabet; a way God identifies Himself in Revelation 22:13 ("I am the Alpha and the Omega, the first and the last, the beginning and the end"); Revelation 1:8; 21:6.

atone, atonement Satisfaction or payment required by the Law on account of our sin.

Baptism A washing with water and the Word for the forgiveness of sins; one of two Sacraments in the Lutheran Church.

belief Something one holds to be true or real.

Bethel Jacob's name for the place where he dreamed about the stairway to heaven; Hebrew for "house of God."

Bible God's inspired Word; a collection of books by many authors about God and His plan for humankind.

birthright In Scripture, a right guaranteeing that the eldest son would become the head of the family and receive a double portion of inheritance upon the death of his father.

blessing An act of asking or receiving divine help, favor, protection, encouragement, or approval.

covenant A formal, binding agreement between two or more people or groups.

covet To sinfully desire to have something or someone belonging to another person.

create God brings into existence everything out of nothing by the power of His Word.

descendant A person who has another person as a parent, grandparent, great-grandparent, and so on.

doctrine A belief or set of beliefs that are taught.

dominion Caring for; ruling over with love and concern.

enmity An attitude of being enemies.

eschatology Study of the end times.

fear The honor and deep reverence of the heart caused by God's grace and mercy.

forgive To excuse for a fault, offense, or sin; God, for Christ's sake, no longer holds our sins against us.

fulfillment The completion or accomplishment of something that was intended or prophesied.

god An idol or anything we worship or place first in our lives that interferes with our love of the true God.

Gospel The Good News about Jesus Christ, who came into the world to save us sinners.

grace The unmerited favor of God—salvation—that He gives us even though we deserve wrath and punishment.

image of God Without sin, perfectly knowing and gladly doing God's will.

inheritance Possessions passed from a parent to a child, usually at the parent's death.

iniquity Sin, wickedness, transgression of God's commandments.

inspiration God breathed the Holy Spirit into the apostles and prophets, which resulted in the writing of the Holy Scriptures.

justify To declare free from blame; we are justified by Jesus' death and resurrection.

kinsman A male relative.

Law What God commands every person to do and not to do, by which He condemns those who break His commandments.

murder To willfully cause the death of a human life out of hatred.

omniscient All-knowing; a trait attributed to God.

original sin The sinful nature of every person born since Adam's sin; the total corruption of our whole human nature, which we have inherited from Adam through our parents.

patriarch "Father," a name used to identify Abraham, Isaac, and Jacob, some ancestors of Jesus.

perish To be destroyed; those who die without faith in Christ will perish eternally.

preserves Keeps, cares for, maintains in good condition.

promise A pledge to do or not to do something specific.

reconcile To repair a broken relationship; to forgive each other and bring peace.

redemption The act of buying back; Jesus redeemed us through His suffering and death on the cross to release us from sin, death, and the power of the devil.

repentance A genuine sorrow toward God on account of sin and belief in Jesus as our Savior.

righteous Right with God; Christ made us right with God by His perfect life, suffering, and death.

sacrifice The offering demanded and provided for by God in payment for sin.

saint A faithful believer in Jesus Christ, either living or already in heaven.

salvation The act of being rescued or saved from sin, death, and the devil for Christ's sake.

sanctification All that the Holy Spirit does through the Word and Sacraments to make us holy.

sin Acts against commandments of God; every thought, desire, word, and deed that is contrary to God's Law.

testament A formal agreement, or covenant, made by God.

translation A change (speech or writing) from one language to another.

triune Three in one; God—the Father, Son, and Holy Spirit—is a triune God.

trust Firm reliance; confident belief; faith; to have faith in; to believe in the honesty and worth of.

unbelief Distrust of God's promises and faithfulness; disbelief in the Gospel of Jesus Christ as our Savior.

worship When God gives us His gifts of forgiveness, life, and salvation in Word and Sacraments, we respond with prayer, praise, and thanksgiving by faith.

wrestle To struggle physically or spiritually.

Bible Words

Upper Elementary—Old Testament 1

Lesson 1   God Creates the World
By [Christ] all things were created, in heaven and on earth, visible and invisible. Colossians 1:16

Lesson 2   God Creates Adam and Eve
I praise You, for I am fearfully and wonderfully made. Psalm 139:14

Lesson 3   Sin Enters the World
For our sake [God] made Him to be sin who knew no sin, so that in Him we might become the righteousness of God. 2 Corinthians 5:21

Lesson 4   Cain and Abel
The Lord . . . is patient toward you, not wishing that any should perish, but that all should reach repentance. 2 Peter 3:9

Lesson 5   Noah and the Flood
The Lord will rescue me from every evil deed and bring me safely into His heavenly kingdom. To Him be the glory forever and ever. Amen. 2 Timothy 4:18

Lesson 6   God's Covenant with Abram
No one can say "Jesus is Lord" except in the Holy Spirit. 1 Corinthians 12:3

Lesson 7   Abraham's Visitors from Heaven
With God all things are possible. Matthew 19:26

Lesson 8   Abraham and Isaac
The next day [John] saw Jesus coming toward him, and said, "Behold, the Lamb of God, who takes away the sin of the world!" John 1:29

Lesson 9   Isaac and Rebekah
The eyes of all look to You, and You give them their food in due season. You open Your hand; You satisfy the desire of every living thing. Psalm 145:15–16

Lesson 10   Jacob and Esau
And I am sure of this, that He who began a good work in you will bring it to completion at the day of Jesus Christ. Philippians 1:6

Lesson 11   Jacob's Dream
How awesome is this place! This is none other than the house of God, and this is the gate of heaven. Genesis 28:17

Lesson 12   Jacob's Family
For I know the plans I have for you, declares the Lord, plans for welfare and not for evil, to give you a future and a hope. Jeremiah 29:11

Lesson 13   Esau Forgives Jacob
For I am sure that neither death nor life, nor angels nor rulers, nor things present nor things to come, nor powers, nor height nor depth, nor anything else in all creation, will be able to separate us from the love of God in Christ Jesus our Lord. Romans 8:38–39